DK EYEWITNESS

T0063855

TOP **10**
BUDAPEST

Top 10 Budapest Highlights

The Top 10 of Everything

CONTENTS

Budapest Area by Area

Streetsmart

Within each Top 10 list in this book, no hierarchy of quality or popularity is implied. All 10 are, in the editor's opinion, of roughly equal merit.

Title page, front cover and spine *The striking main tower of the Fisherman's Bastion with the Danube in the distance*
Back cover, clockwise from top left
The Freedom Bridge; Budapest Skyline; St Stephen's Basilica; Fisherman's Bastion; crowded Váci Street

The rapid rate at which the world is changing is constantly keeping the DK Eyewitness team on our toes. While we've worked hard to ensure that this edition of Budapest is accurate and up-to-date, we know that opening hours alter, standards shift, prices fluctuate, places close and new ones pop up in their stead. So, if you notice we've got something wrong or left something out, we want to hear about it. Please get in touch at **travelguides@dk.com**

Welcome to
Budapest

Bestriding the Danube, Hungary's capital is not one city but two. Buda, with its medieval streets and imperial palaces, rises on the west side of the river; Pest, the commercial and political hub of modern Hungary, lines the east. Together they make up one of Europe's most enchanting cities. With DK Eyewitness Top 10 Budapest, it's yours to explore.

Buda is dominated by the **Castle District**, which sits atop a rocky crag overlooking the Danube. This UNESCO World Heritage Site is crisscrossed by a web of winding lanes lined with old-world cafés and restaurants. It has some of the city's most renowned sights, including the imposing **Royal Palace** and the striking **Mátyás Church**. South of here lies leafy **Gellért Hill**, dotted with monuments and thermal baths, including the opulent Byzantine **Rudas Baths** and stunning Secessionist **Gellért Hotel and Baths Complex**. Much of Buda can be explored on foot, while a network of funiculars, historic trains and chairlifts offer access to the rolling **Buda Hills** beyond.

Linking Buda to Pest is the mighty **Chain Bridge**; completed in 1849, it shifted the heart of the city from one bank of the Danube to the other. Since then, Pest has become Budapest's dynamic heart, not least in the central shopping and entertainment district around **Váci Street**. This half of the city is also home to the sprawling **City Park** and iconic **Heroes' Square**, as well as the historic **Jewish Quarter**, known for its impressive **Great Synagogue**.

Whether you're visiting for a weekend or a week, our Top 10 guide brings together the best of everything the city has to offer, from the grandeur of **Buda** to the bustle of **Pest**. The guide has useful tips throughout, from seeking out what's free to finding places off the beaten track, plus eight easy-to-follow itineraries, designed to tie together a clutch of sights in a short space of time. Add inspiring photography and detailed maps, and you've got the essential pocket-sized travel companion. **Enjoy the book, and enjoy Budapest**.

Clockwise from top: **Interior of the Hungarian National Museum, carvings on the Fishermen's Bastion, ceiling of the Hungarian State Opera, Danube façade of the Parliament, statue of a lion on Chain Bridge, Ornate lace, Centenary Monument on Margaret Island**

Exploring Budapest

Budapest is packed with things to see and do. Whether you have just a couple of days to explore it or more time, you'll want to make every minute count. To help you do just that, here are two sightseeing itineraries covering the main highlights of Hungary's fascinating capital city.

Fishermen's Bastion, set high on Castle Hill, offers the best view of the city from its conical turrets.

To Elizabeth
Lookout Tower 5km (3 miles)
see inset map

BUS

Batthyány
Square

VÍZIVÁROS

Mátyás
Church

St Mary
Magdalene

Fishermen's
Bastion

Lords'
Street

Funicul

Royal
Palace

Hungarian
National Gallery

Castle Museu

TABÁ

TRAM

Key
— Two-day itinerary
— Four-day itinerary

Two Days in Budapest

Day ❶
MORNING
Ride the **Castle Hill Funicular** *(see p49)* up to the Castle District and stroll the grounds of the **Royal Palace** *(see p69)* before seeing the fantastic collection of Secession art at the **Hungarian National Gallery** *(see pp26–9)*.
AFTERNOON
Explore medieval Buda: pretty **Lords' Street** *(see p70)*, **Mátyás Church** *(see pp30–31)* and the ruined **Church of St Mary Magdalene** *(see p71)*. Don't miss views across the Danube from the **Fishermen's Bastion** *(see p70)*.

Day ❷
MORNING
Spend some time in the **Hungarian National Museum** *(see pp34–5)* before exploring **Váci Street** *(see pp18–19)*.
AFTERNOON
Take a guided tour of the **Hungarian Parliament** *(see pp12–13)* and visit **St Stephen's Basilica** *(see pp16–17)*. Afterwards, watch a show at the **Hungarian State Opera** *(see pp32–3)*.

Four Days in Budapest

Day ❶
MORNING
Visit **Margaret Island** *(see pp22–3)*, a peaceful park situated in the middle of the Danube. Be sure not to miss the Japanese Garden.
AFTERNOON
Explore the Castle District, especially **Lords' Street** *(see p70)* and **Mátyás Church** *(see pp30–31)*, and enjoy the views from the **Fishermen's Bastion** *(see p70)*. Spend the evening relaxing at the **Gellért Hotel and Baths Complex** *(see pp20–21)*.

Day ❷
MORNING
Enjoy coffee at **Gerbeaud Cukrászda** *(see p57)* on **Vörösmarty Square** *(see p89)* before strolling along **Váci Street** *(see pp18–19)*. Don't miss the **Inner City Parish Church** *(see p42)*.

The Royal Palace, or Castle, is home to several museums, including the world-class Hungarian National Gallery.

Day ❸
MORNING
Stroll along the Pest embankment to the **Hungarian Parliament** *(see pp12–13)*, pausing at the moving *Shoes on the Danube* memorial *(see p46)*. Afterwards, explore the lovely **St Stephen's Basilica** *(see pp16–17)*, in which the Holy Right Hand of the eponymous saint resides.

AFTERNOON
The Byzantine-inspired **Great Synagogue** *(see pp36–7)* and its Hungarian Jewish Museum *(see p44)* are a must-see. After your visit, take a tour of the **Hungarian State Opera** *(see pp32–3)* and catch an evening performance.

Day ❹
MORNING
Start your day at the **Royal Palace** *(see p69)*, visiting both the **Hungarian National Gallery** *(see pp26–9)* and the **Castle Museum** *(see p69)*.
AFTERNOON
Head into the **Buda Hills** *(see p101)* via the chair lift to the top of **János Hill** *(see p103)*. Take a ride on the unique **Children's Railway** *(see p52)* to the Elizabeth Lookout Tower. Climb to the top for great views of the city.

AFTERNOON
Allow yourself the luxury of a full afternoon to take in all that the superb **Hungarian National Museum** *(see pp34–5)* has to offer.

Top 10 Budapest Highlights

The Grand Staircase of the
Hungarian Parliament

🔟 Budapest Highlights

One part of the Habsburg triumvirate of Budapest, Vienna and Prague, the Hungarian capital is undeniably grand. Comprising two separate towns – hilly Buda on the Danube's western bank and flat Pest on the eastern bank – this is a city rich in historical sights.

① Hungarian Parliament

Viewed from the opposite bank of the Danube, the façade of the Hungarian Parliament is one of Budapest's defining sights. Its chambers contain magnificent treasures *(see pp12–15)*.

St Stephen's Basilica ②

With its 96-m- (315-ft-) high dome visible from all over the city, St Stephen's Basilica houses the city's most unusual relic – the mummified forearm of St Stephen (King István) *(see pp16–17)*.

③ Váci Street

For centuries, Váci Street has been the centre of the Hungarian commercial world, and it remains Budapest's retail and social hub *(see pp18–19)*.

Gellért Hotel and Baths Complex ④

Budapest is famous for its numerous thermal baths, and the best are the indoor and outdoor pools at the legendary Gellért Hotel *(see pp20–21)*.

⑤ Margaret Island

Isolated until the 19th century and long a retreat for religious contemplation, the lush and still-secluded Margaret Island is an ideal place for a peaceful stroll *(see pp22–3)*.

⑥ Hungarian National Gallery

The six permanent exhibitions spread throughout much of Budapest's Royal Palace present the most valuable collection of Hungarian art in the world *(see pp26–9).*

Mátyás Church ⑦

The coronation church of the Hungarian kings, with its Gothic spire towering above much of Upper Buda, is as impressive close up as it is from afar *(see pp30–31).*

⑧ Hungarian State Opera

Built to rival the opera houses of Vienna and Dresden, the sublime Hungarian State Opera stages world-class performances *(see pp32–3).*

⑩ Great Synagogue

The largest of its kind in Europe, Budapest's Great Synagogue *(see pp36–7)* was built in a Byzantine-Moorish style. It also houses the Hungarian Jewish Museum *(see p44).*

⑨ Hungarian National Museum

A treasure-trove of exhibits and artifacts from every period of Hungary's turbulent history *(see pp34–5).*

TOP10 ⭐ Hungarian Parliament

In 1846, the Hungarian poet Mihály Vörösmarty wrote with some desperation that "the motherland has no home". When Hungary opened its magnificent Parliament building after decades of construction in 1902, it not only had a home, but one of the finest Neo-Gothic buildings in Europe. The largest parliament building in the world at the time, it stood as a symbol of Hungarian self-confidence in the early 20th century. Designed by Imre Steindl, it is one of Budapest's defining landmarks, surpassed only by the Royal Palace.

1 Cross-Danube Vista
Sensational close up, the Hungarian Parliament is arguably even better from afar. Set along the banks of the Danube **(below)**, its spires and symmetry can be admired from the other side of the river.

2 Main Entrance
Inspired by London's Houses of Parliament, and built with no expense spared, the main entrance is guarded by two lions sculpted by Béla Markup and József Somogyi.

3 Crown Jewels
Spirited out of Hungary after World War II – and stored in Fort Knox, USA, until 1978 – the Crown of St Stephen and the Royal Sceptre are now kept in the Domed Hall.

4 National Assembly Hall
The Hungarian Lower House is where Parliament sits. The bullet hole above the lectern dates from 1912, when an assassin tried to kill the speaker, István Tisza.

5 Grand Staircase
The sumptuous main staircase **(left)** is decorated with three outstanding ceiling frescoes. These include Károly Lotz's *Glorification of Hungary*, depicting scenes from the lives of the country's kings and saints.

6 Delegation Room

A relic of the Dual Monarchy (see p76), this was where parliamentarians met delegates of the ministries. Its walls have artworks by Andor Dudits, while the ceiling paintings, *Wisdom* and *Fortitude*, are by Károly Lotz.

7 Domed Hall

The spiritual heart of the building, the Domed Hall **(right)** was once used to host joint sessions of Parliament. Each of the 16 pillars supporting the dome features a statue of a Hungarian king or queen (see pp14–15). The hall is used for official ceremonies.

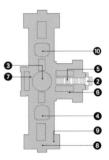

8 The Conquest

The finest work of art here is Munkácsy's *The Conquest*. Originally intended for the Chamber of Commons, it was rejected as it was thought to misrepresent the first contact between the invading Magyars and Pannonian tribes as a peaceful meeting, rather than a conquest.

IMRE STEINDL

Before submitting his entry for the competition to design Hungary's Parliament, Imre Steindl also submitted designs for a proposed parliament in Berlin. His plans were rejected, and the winning entry was, of course, Paul Wallot's Reichstag. Berlin's loss was Hungary's gain as Steindl's vision resulted in a masterpiece. He is remembered by a bust, cast by Alajos Stróbl, on the main staircase.

Hungarian Parliament

NEED TO KNOW

MAP J1 ■ V, Kossuth Lajos tér 1–3
■ 06 1 441 49 04; 06 1 441 44 15
■ www.parlament.hu

Open 8am–4pm daily
Head to the visitor centre
for more information

Adm Ft3,500 for EU citizens
and Ft6,700 for all others

■ The only way you can see all the attractions in the building is via a guided tour when Parliament is not in session.

■ To book a ticket, visit the website www.jegymester.hu/parlament.

■ There is no café on the premises, but there is one in the visitor centre, and there are several other options in the surrounding area.

9 Prime Minister's Office

The prime minister's office is closed to visitors, but you can admire its reception rooms, with paintings by Géza Udvary and Antal Diósy.

10 Congress Hall

Unused for legislation since 1944, when Hungary became a unicameral state, the former Hungarian Upper House **(above)** has a rich interior with a painting by Zsigmond Vajda of the monk Astrik handing St Stephen his crown.

Domed Hall Statues

Statue of Prince Árpád

1 Prince Árpád

Prince Árpád was chosen as the leader of the Magyar tribes shortly after they settled on the Pannonian plains in AD 896. The Magyars migrated from the Ural mountains in present-day Russia.

2 St Stephen

St Stephen (István) was elected Duke of the Magyars in AD 997. He adopted Christianity soon after, and was crowned king by Pope Sylvester II in 1001.

3 St Ladislaus

Hungary's ruler from 1077 to 1095, Ladislaus (László I) was victorious against the Turks and the Cumans, and annexed Croatia in 1092.

4 András II

The son of King Béla III and brother of Emeric (Imre), András II was crowned in 1205. He expanded the Magyar state eastwards, conquering swathes of Transylvania and encouraging vast numbers of Magyars to settle in the region.

5 Béla IV

Defeated by the Tatars in 1241, Béla IV survived to rebuild Hungary after the Tatars left the country in ashes a year later. His patient rebuilding of the nation over the next 25 years elevated him to greatness.

6 Louis I

Crowned in 1342, Louis (Lajos) the Great reigned for 40 years, expanding the Magyar kingdom with victories over Venice and Dalmatia between 1357 and 1358. In 1370, he formed a political union with Poland after the death of his uncle, the Polish king Casimir III, and ruled as sovereign of both, until his death in 1382.

7 János Hunyadi

János Hunyadi was born to a Romanian family of Vlach nobles who had served the Hungarian king Sigismund (Zsigmond). A gifted commander, Hunyadi became the ruler of Transylvania in 1441, and then Governor of Hungary in 1446. He is remembered for defeating the Turks in the Battle of Belgrade in 1456.

8 Mátyás Corvinus

The second son of János, Mátyás was born in Cluj-Napoca, Transylvania, and is generally considered to be the greatest of all Hungarian kings. Crowned in 1458 at the age of 15, he was a Renaissance man who valued the sciences, arts and architecture, and invited foreign writers, humanists, musicians and

Domed Hall Statues

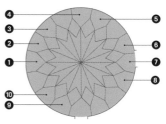

artists to his court. The first Hungarian printing press and library were founded during his 32-year reign.

9 Charles III

In 1687, Hungary finally succumbed to Austrian domination and renounced its right to elect its own king. The Habsburgs inherited the throne and Charles VI, the last Holy Roman Emperor of the direct Habsburg line, became Charles VI King of Bohemia and Charles III King of Hungary. The king spent much of his reign ensuring that his daughter, Maria Theresa, would succeed him.

Interior of the Domed Hall

10 Maria Theresa

Maria Theresa acceded to the throne in 1740, cementing Hungary's position as an integral part of the Habsburg Empire. Buda became an imperial city and the magnificent Habsburg Royal Palace was built during the Queen's reign. The city became a centre of Central European art, second only to Vienna. Maria ruled Hungary until her death in 1780.

THE DOMED HALL

The first section of the Parliament to be completed was the Domed Hall in 1896. It was used for a special session of Parliament held during Budapest's Millennium Celebrations. The 16-sided dome – which, at 96 m (315 ft), is the same height as that of St Stephen's Basilica – was designed to convey a sense of amplified space. Each of the 16 pillars supporting the dome bears the statue and coat of arms of a significant Hungarian ruler. Apart from the ten dignitaries mentioned above, the six remaining statues represent (in a clockwise direction) Könyves Kálmán, András III, István Báthory, István Bocskai, Gábor Bethlen and Leopold II.

Magnificent ceiling of the Domed Hall

TOP 10 DATES IN THE PARLIAMENT'S HISTORY

1 1885 Foundation stone laid, 12 Oct

2 1896 First session of Parliament, 15 Mar

3 1902 Parliament building completed

4 1912 Assassin attempts to shoot speaker, 4 Jun

5 1920 Treaty of Trianon strips Hungary of two-thirds of its territory, 4 Jun

6 1944 Hungary becomes a unicameral republic

7 1956 Armed uprising against Soviet rule, 23 Oct. Soviet tanks intervene, a new government is set up

8 1958 Execution of Prime Minister Imre Nagy, 16 Jun

9 1989 Proclaimed a republic and multi-party elections allowed by Communists, 23 Oct

10 1990 MPs take their seats after post-Communist elections, 2 May

🔟⭐ St Stephen's Basilica

More than worthy of St Stephen, the Basilica that carries his name is visible from all over Budapest. Splendidly lit in the evening, it is perhaps the most photographed sight in the city. The dome, at 96 m (315 ft), is the same height as that of Parliament, as it represents the year 1896 – the 1000th anniversary of the Magyars in Hungary. It was built between 1851 and 1905 in the form of a Greek cross, and is the work of three architects – József Hild, Miklós Ybl and József Kauser.

1 Main Altar

A life-size marble statue of St Stephen (King István), by sculptor Alajos Stróbl, dominates the main altar **(below)** of the Basilica. On either side, fine paintings by the 19th-century artist Gyula Benczúr depict scenes from the saint-king's life.

4 Dome and Mosaics

The Neo-Renaissance dome was designed by Miklós Ybl in 1867 after the original dome – designed by József Hild – caved in due to poor workmanship and materials. It is decorated with mosaics **(right)** by Károly Lotz. A viewing platform above the cupola offers panoramic views of the city; it is reached by a lift and stairs.

2 Main Entrance

"I am the way and the truth and the life" proclaims the Latin inscription above the Basilica's main entrance. Situated above the inscription are several statues of Hungarian saints paying homage to the Virgin Mary and the infant Jesus.

5 North Tower

The 9,144-kg (9-ton) bell in the North Tower **(below)** was paid for by German Catholics, who were ashamed that the Nazis had looted the original at the end of World War II during their retreat from Budapest. The original bell was never traced.

3 St Gellért and St Emeric

Alajos Stróbl carved the statue of St Gellért and his pupil, St Emeric (St Stephen's son, Imre), that stands in a small nave in the centre of the main hall. Opposite, the statue of St Elizabeth is by Károly Senyei.

6 Treasury

A replica of the holy Hungarian crown forms the centrepiece of a small collection of religious jewellery. The original crown of St Stephen (see p14) is now kept in the Domed Hall of the Hungarian Parliament (see pp12–15). Gifts to Hungarian kings from a succession of popes are also on display here.

7 Holy Right Hand

The mummified forearm of St Stephen **(left)** is displayed in the Holy Right Hand Chapel near the main altar. It was taken to Dubrovnik in Croatia by Béla IV in the 13th century to protect it from the Tatars. After time in Vienna and at the Royal Palace in Buda, it was brought here on 20 August 1945 – St Stephen's Day.

ORGAN CONCERTS

The Basilica's organ was made by Angster & Sons of Pécs, and installed in 1904. At the time, it was considered the world's finest. The organ was enlarged in 1934, and today comprises no fewer than 5,898 pipes. You can hear it at special organ concerts, which are held in the Basilica from time to time.

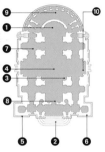

St Stephen's Basilica

10 Gyula Benczúr Painting

The painting *St Stephen*, by Gyula Benczúr, is one of the most important works in the Hungarian artistic cannon. It portrays the king – who died without an heir – proffering the care of the country and the crown to the Virgin Mary.

8 Main Portal

The oak front door is decorated with medallions that depict the heads of the 12 Apostles. Despite the door's age the carvings remain an impressive sight.

9 Figures of the 12 Apostles

The Basilica's rear colonnade has 12 superb statues by Leó Feszler representing the 12 Apostles. Below is a fine Neo-Classical loggia.

NEED TO KNOW

MAP L2 ■ V, Szent István tér ■ 06 1 317 28 59

Basilica: 9am–7pm Mon–Sat, 7:45am–7pm Sun

Treasury and Dome: 10am–6:30pm daily (to 5:30pm Apr–May & Oct, to 4:30pm Nov–Mar)

Adm Ft2,000 for Treasury and Dome

Guided tours: 9:30am–4pm daily by appt (email turizmus@basilica.hu); Adm Ft12,700

Donations to the main church are welcome.

■ Every year on St Stephen's Day (20 Aug), the Holy Right Hand is carried by the Basilica's priests past large crowds of people who gather in front of the Basilica. Arrive early to witness the spectacle.

■ Choose from a number of restaurants and cafés located opposite the Basilica's main entrance.

TOP10 ⭐ Váci Street

Váci Street, or Váci utca, is one of the city's best-known streets. With two parts – the northern end for shopping and the southern end for drinking and eating – it buzzes with life day and night, and acts as the city's commercial and social hub. Many buildings here date from the 19th and early 20th century. Most of the street is pedestrianized apart from where it is bisected by the access road to Elizabeth Bridge. To get a real feel of the street, you should stroll down its full length.

1 Gerbeaud Cukrászda

This is the most famous coffee house in Budapest. Since 1858, Gerbeaud Cukrászda **(above)** has been known for its richly decorated interior *(see p57)*. Expect it to be busy.

2 Vörösmarty Square Metro Station

The tiled walls, wooden booths and platforms of this immaculate 1903 station remind one why underground railways were considered glamorous. The tiny yellow trains are enchanting too.

3 Philanthia

Opened in 1905, this Secession-style florist now occupies part of the Neo-Classical block at No. 9. The block was built in 1840 by József Hild and was once occupied by the Inn of the Seven Electors, which had a large ballroom/concert hall where a 12-year-old Franc Liszt performed.

4 The Promenade

Walk the full length of Váci Street **(right)** from Vörösmarty Square to Vámház körút and on your way take in the atmosphere, the bustle and the stunning architecture of the street's buildings. You won't be alone during the summer, but the crowds are a part of the appeal.

5 Klotild Palaces

Forming a splendid entrance to Elizabeth Bridge, the twin Klotild Palaces **(below)** were commissioned by Archduchess Klotild, daughter-in-law of Emperor Franz József, and finished in 1902. Their interiors are mostly shops or offices. They also house the luxurious Buddha-Bar Hotel *(see p115)*.

6 Thonet House

Built from 1888 to 1890 by Ödön Lechner and Gyula Pártos, Thonet House once belonged to a wealthy family. Zsolnay ceramics **(right)** adorn the walls, while the shop sells exclusive crystal.

7 St Michael's City Church

First built around 1230, St Michael's City Church **(left)** was devastated by the Turks in 1541, rebuilt in 1701 and renovated between 1964 and 1968. Its plain exterior belies a rich interior, including a fine gold pulpit and dome.

VÁCI STREET

The name of Budapest's famous street has simple origins. The street was once the main road linking Pest to the town of Vác *(see p65)*, 40 km (25 miles) north of Budapest. The gate leading to Vác used to stand at Váci utca No. 3.

8 Palais Herend

Herend ceramics are famous for their intricacy and quality. This outlet is one of the few places you can be sure of finding the genuine article.

9 Central Market Hall

Budapest's largest market *(see p59)* has a number of stalls on the ground floor selling vegetables, fish and cheese. Specialities are spicy *kolbász* salami and sheep's cheese. Upper-level stalls sell local crafts.

10 1000 Tea

Váci Street has lots of places to eat, drink and while away the hours, but a relaxing oasis away from the hustle and bustle is 1000 Tea. This quiet café has a selection of loose-leaf teas from all over the world. It is a great place to rest after a day's shopping.

NEED TO KNOW

MAP C4-C5

Gerbeaud Cukrászda: V, Vörösmarty tér 7-8; 06 1 429 90 00; open 9am–9pm daily; www.gerbeaud.hu

Philanthia: V, Váci utca 9; 0670 933 22 66

Thonet House: V, Váci utca 11

Palais Herend: V, József Nádor tér 10-11; 06 20 241 57 36; open 10am–6pm Mon–Fri, 10am–2pm Sat

1000 Tea: V, Váci utca 65; www.1000tea.hu

▪ As with all extremely busy tourist streets, beware of pickpockets and be cautious of anyone approaching you to ask for directions.

▪ Most places here can be expensive, and some have dubious pricing policies. Make sure prices are clearly indicated on the menu and check your bill carefully.

Váci Street

🔟⭐ Gellért Hotel and Baths Complex

This is the finest of all of Budapest's great bath houses. Its main swimming pool is an excellent example of Neo-Classical architecture in Hungary, and is the ideal place to enjoy Budapest's therapeutic waters. The hotel itself is a fine modernist Secessionist piece built between 1912 and 1918. The building was damaged by heavy bombing in World War II and rebuilt in the late 1940s.

1 Façade
The Gellert's Secession-era façade **(below)** reflects the self-confidence of the era in which it was constructed – during the final phase of the Habsburg Empire, when Hungary was poised on the verge of independence.

2 Hotel's Main Entrance Hall
With elaborate mosaics and over-the-top statues, the hotel's entrance hall is a leap into the past. The staff are patient with visitors who just want to admire the scene.

Main Staircase 3
The stained-glass windows **(right)** on the staircase landings were designed by Gyula Bozó. They illustrate a legend about a magic stag, recorded in János Arany's poetry.

4 Main Swimming Pool
The stunning Neo-Classical main pool **(above)** is the finest part of the Gellért Baths. Surrounded by high galleries and marble columns, it is decorated with colourful mosaics. Note that it is obligatory to wear a swimming cap in this part of the baths.

5 Steam Rooms and Saunas
In addition to the healing waters of the pools, the Gellért also has an extensive range of steam rooms (also known as wet saunas) and traditional Finnish saunas (sometimes called dry saunas). The entrance fee to both of these is included in the price of a standard baths ticket.

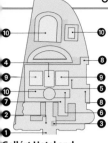

Gellért Hotel and Baths Complex

7 Private Baths

For an extra fee, guests can reserve a private thermal bath (book in advance). The private bath is designed for couples and the experience includes champagne, Szamos marzipan dessert and access to a private sauna.

8 Eastern-Style Towers

Although the Gellért is primarily a Secessionist building, its cylindrical, Eastern-style towers commemorate the earlier Turkish baths that stood on this site.

9 Thermal Baths

The medicinal waters here were first discovered in the 13th century during the reign of King András II. In the Middle Ages, a hospital was built on this spot. Today, there is a great network of thermal baths **(right)** at various temperatures. Massages and private baths are available.

HEALING WATERS

Although Budapest is known for its baths, few visitors realize the major role they play in city life, and how much faith the locals place in the healing properties of their waters. For many of the city's older residents, the baths remain as important as they were under the Ottomans, who first developed the potential of Budapest's astonishing 120-odd thermal springs. Most of the city's thermal waters contain high levels of sulphur, and are said to be especially effective in treating rheumatism, arthritis and even Parkinson's disease.

6 Bath Foyers

There are three foyers at the entrance to the baths. The central foyer's glass roof is the highlight, but the floors, walls, statuettes and benches of the others are also marvellous. You can admire them without paying to enter.

10 Outdoor Pools

During the summer, bathers head to the outdoor pools and sun terraces. The main outdoor pool was one of the first in the world to have an artificial wave mechanism, which is still in use today.

NEED TO KNOW

MAP L6

Danubius Hotel Gellért: XI, Szent Gellért tér 1; 06 1 889 55 00; closed for renovation; www.danubius hotels.com/gellert

Gellért Baths: XI, Kelen-hegyi út 4; 06 1 466 61 66; open 9am–7pm daily; adm Ft5,900 weekdays, Ft6,200 weekends (lockers are cheaper than cabins; www.gellertbath.hu

■ Refuel after a day at the baths by ordering one of the huge platters of tapas at Palack Borbar *(see p79),* just across the street. There are some great wines on offer, too.

■ Swimming costumes and towels can be hired at the baths but are costly, so it's best to bring your own.

■ Standard entry at Gellért includes access to the baths, swimming pool, sauna and steam room. Special treatments incur an additional cost.

TOP 10 ⭐ Margaret Island

Inhabited since Roman times, Margaret Island (Margitsziget) is a tranquil, green oasis in the middle of the Danube. It is named after Princess Margit, daughter of King Béla IV, who spent most of her life in the island's convent in the 13th century. It was also a popular hunting ground for medieval kings. The island has served as Budapest's playground since 1869.

2 Franciscan Church

The secluded ruins of the 14th-century Franciscan church **(left)** lie in the island's centre. Though there is very little left to admire, it still has a fine arched window and a staircase.

3 St Michael's Church

The oldest building on Margaret Island, St Michael's Church was founded in the 11th century, but was devastated by the Turks in 1541. Visitors today can see a 1930s reconstruction, which used materials salvaged from the original building.

5 Japanese Garden

The most delightful spot on the island is the Japanese Garden **(below)** at the northern end, with lily pools, rock gardens and waterfalls.

1 Dominican Convent

One of the island's most important monuments is the ruin of a 13th-century Dominican convent. This was founded by Béla IV, whose daughter Margit came to live here in 1251. A plaque in the church marks the spot where she is buried.

4 Centenary Monument

The striking Modernist Centenary Monument **(left)** was installed in 1973 to commemorate the unification of Buda, Óbuda and Pest to form Budapest in 1873.

NEED TO KNOW

MAP B1 ■ XIII, Margaret Island (Margitsziget)

■ The easiest way to get to Margaret Island is by bus No. 26 from Nyugati Station. However, the most enjoyable way is by boat. In summer, public transport boats marked D12 run along the Danube, stopping twice at the island, near the Centenary Monument and the hotels in the north. Check the timetable at bkk.hu/en.

■ For lunch, head to Palatinus Strand for *lángos* (fried salty dough with toppings) and hot dogs. For a formal meal, visit the Ensana Thermal Margaret Island.

6 Water Tower

Built in 1911, this UNESCO-protected Water Tower (below), also serves as an exhibition hall during the summer season. It stands 57 m (187 ft) high, and a gallery offers panoramic views of the island.

8 Musical Fountain

From March to October, this fountain leaps into action morning and night, shooting water in time to a classical piece or pop song. Coloured lights are added for evening performances.

PRINCESS MARGIT (MARGARET)

After the horrors of the Mongol invasion and subsequent destruction of Budapest from 1241 to 1242, a desperate King Béla IV offered to give his daughter to God if, in return, he would ensure that the Mongols never returned. In 1251, Béla made good his vow and sent his 9-year-old daughter Margit to the island's convent, where she stayed for the rest of her life. The Mongols never returned.

Margaret Island

10 Bodor Well

The unusual musical Bodor Well (below) is a copy of a long-destroyed well built in 1820 in Târgu Mures, Romania. This copy dates from 1936 and plays recorded music on the hour.

7 Palatinus Strand

Opened in 1919, the city's largest outdoor pool complex buzzes from dawn to dusk, as people enjoy the therapeutic waters pumped from the island's thermal springs (see p49). There are water slides and special pools for the kids.

9 Ensana Thermal Margaret Island

This legendary hotel designed by Miklós Ybl opened in 1872. For years, it was the most fashionable in the city, attracting aristocracy from all over Europe. Today, it has been joined by a sister spa (see p49).

Following pages The Chain Bridge over the Danube

🔟 ⭐ Hungarian National Gallery

The treasure-trove that is the Hungarian National Gallery has been housed in the Royal Palace since 1975, when a large section of the building was given over to it. It displays pieces from medieval times to the present day, and there are six permanent exhibitions that present the cream of Hungarian fine arts. The Gallery's collection is shared with the Museum of Fine Arts (see p95), and is especially strong in Secession art (see p29).

1 The Recapture of Buda Castle in 1686
Gyula Benczúr painted this masterpiece **(below)** for the 1896 Millennium Celebrations. It was meant to emphasize the need for Austro-Hungarian rule by showing that Hungary was only freed from Turkish rule thanks to Karl of Lotharingia and Eugene of Savoy.

2 Picnic in May
Painted from memory in 1873 by Pál Szinyei-Merse, *Picnic in May* is close to the French Impressionist style. The figure lying with his back towards us is the artist himself.

3 Women of Eger
Besides his fine portrait work, Bertalan Székely painted historical works featuring simple, heroic female figures in a romantic style. *Women of Eger* (1867), portrays the women of the town defending Eger Castle against the Turks.

4 Habsburg Crypt
This Crypt, with the exquisite sarcophagus of Palatine Archduke Joseph, is a Neo-Classical warren of black-and-white marble and gold leaf. It can only be seen on a guided tour.

5 Great Throne Room
An entire room of the Gallery is devoted to 15th- and 16th-century Gothic altarpieces. The best, painted in 1520, depict St Anne and St John the Baptist from a church in Kisszeben (Sabinov, in present-day Slovakia).

6 The Visitation
Nothing is known about Master MS, who was the chief exponent of late Gothic painting in Hungary. His best work **(above)**, dated 1500–10, depicts the Virgin Mary meeting St Elizabeth.

7 The Yawning Apprentice
The Yawning Apprentice (1867) **(below)** is a well-known and much-loved work by Hungary's finest Realist, Mihály Munkácsy. It is celebrated for its extraordinary detail.

8 Main Entrance
Part of the 18th-century Maria Theresa Palace, the late Baroque façade has an eclectic range of influences.

Birdsong 9

Károly Ferenczy was one of Hungary's finest artists at the turn of the 19th century. *Birdsong* **(right)**, painted in 1893, is one of his best works. It sees him move away from the "delicate naturalism" made famous by French artists like Jules Bastien-Lepage and towards his own distinct style.

MIHÁLY MUNKÁCSY

Regarded as Hungary's finest artist, Mihály Munkácsy began his career making finished woodwork. After completing his first major painting in 1869, when he was just 25, he moved to Paris, where he painted a series of masterpieces including *The Churning Woman* and *Woman Carrying Brushwood*, both now in the National Gallery. He died in 1900 at the age of 55 in Paris.

Hungarian National Gallery Floorplan

The Visitation 6

9 Birdsong

10 Woman Bathing

3 Women of Eger

2 Picnic in May

Key to Floorplan
- Ground floor
- 1st floor
- 2nd floor
- 3rd floor

5 Great Throne Room

Main Entrance 8

4 Habsburg Crypt

1 The Recapture of Buda Castle in 1686

7 The Yawning Apprentice

10 Woman Bathing

Nudes were a speciality of Károly Lotz, who painted this particularly sensuous figure in 1901. A fine example of academic painting, it evokes the style of the French artist, Ingres. Lotz is also known for the murals in the Hungarian Parliament *(see pp12–14)*.

NEED TO KNOW

MAP H4 ■ Royal Palace buildings A, B, C and D ■ 06 20 439 73 31 ■ www.mng.hu

Open 10am–6pm Tue–Sun

Adm Ft3,200; audio guide in English available for select collections, Ft900

■ The gallery can be visited for free on 15 March, 20 August & 23 October (national holidays).

■ Allow yourself at least three hours to see the entire collection.

Gallery Guide

Early stone and Gothic works are on the ground floor. Late Gothic, Renaissance and Baroque, and 19th-century works are on first floor. Second floor has 20th-century exhibits. The top floor has Hungarian works post 1945.

Secession Works in the Gallery

① Woman in a White-Spotted Dress

József Rippl-Rónai (1861–1927) was one of the three most important artists of the Secession movement. He studied for several years in Paris, at a time when the Art Nouveau movement was starting to flourish. His masterpiece *Woman in a White-Spotted Dress* (1889) depicts the somewhat affected pose of a model apparently caught off-guard. It is said to have been the first Secession-style work painted in Hungary.

Woman in a White-Spotted Dress

② Woman with a Birdcage

An early painting by Rippl-Rónai, *Woman with a Birdcage* (1892) is renowned for its marvellous use of contrast – note the white of the girl's hands compared to the blurred, dark background. The slightly contrived pose of the model holding the cage is a trademark of the artist.

③ The Manor House at Körtvélyes

Rippl-Rónai visited Italy in 1904 and was fascinated by the decorative mosaics he saw in many homes. This 1907 work anticipates his shift from soft brushwork to bolder strokes, which would culminate in the paintings of his later years.

The Manor House at Körtvélyes

④ Girls Getting Dressed

This 1912 Rippl-Rónai work shows the progression of his characteristic "corn kernels" style, where his brushstrokes became bolder and his colours brighter. The somewhat awkward pose of the girl on the left betrays the artist's love of playing with the viewer's perception.

⑤ The Golden Age

The second of Hungary's great Secessionist triumvirate, János Vaszary (1867–1939) oscillated between Art Nouveau and Post-Impressionism. His best work is probably this 1898 rendition of a couple yearning for a lost paradise.

Fancy Dress Ball

⑥ Fancy Dress Ball

Vaszary's brightly coloured 1907 portrayal of Budapest society has a touch of decadence. The painting is also known as *Masquerade Ball*.

⑦ Breakfast in the Open Air

This 1907 painting by Vaszary makes fabulous use of light and colour, and showcases the artist's bold brushwork. Ostensibly a flattering portrayal of a Budapest high society family at breakfast, the youngest child's troubled look suggests hidden problems and adds depth to the work.

8 Riders in the Park

Dating from 1919, this is another fine example of late Secessionist painting by Vaszary, with sharp brushstrokes and high contrast colours. The influence of Matisse, whom he knew from his sojourns in Paris, is clearly visible in this work.

9 The Garden of the Magician

Lajos Gulácsy (1882–1932) was the youngest

The Garden of the Magician

of Hungary's famous Secessionist trio. His style and approach were greatly influenced by spending 13 years in Italy, where he painted *The Garden of the Magician*. His output also shows echoes of the English Pre-Raphaelites, particularly the work of Dante Gabriel Rossetti.

10 Self-Portrait with Hat

Lajos Gulácsy's *Self-Portrait with Hat* (1912) reinforces his rather detached view of the world and, perhaps, his lack of belief in his own abilities. In the painting, his face is wearing an anxious and vulnerable expression.

THE SECESSION

From its quiet beginnings among avant-garde artists in Vienna in the late 1880s, until it gave way to Art Deco in the 1920s, the Secession movement was an attempt to break away from the romantic historicism of 19th-century art. It tried to find new inspiration in the distant past; in Hungary it explored the bold colours of Transylvanian folk art. Often characterized by fantastical designs, bright colours and stylized forms, the movement repossessed art from the nationalists. It encompassed all forms of the decorative and visual arts, from painting and sculpture to interior design. It is represented in the paintings of the National Gallery, in the Zsolnay ceramics all round the city and, above all, in the architecture of the day.

TOP 10 SECESSIONIST BUILDINGS

1 Four Seasons Hotel Gresham Palace *(Map K3)*

2 Gellért Hotel and Baths Complex *(Map L6)*

3 Museum of Applied Arts *(Map D5)*

4 Geology Institute *(Map F3)*

5 Hungarian National Bank *(Map K2)*

6 Post Office Savings Bank *(Map L2)*

7 Városliget Calvinist Church *(Map E3)*

8 Franz Liszt Academy of Music *(Map D3)*

9 New York Palace *(Map D4)*

10 New Theatre *(Map M2)*

Gresham Palace is now a hotel *(see p83 & p116)*, and is famous for its Secessionist stained glass and mosaics.

TOP 10 ⭐ Mátyás Church

The profusion of architectural styles in Mátyás Church reveals the building's and the city's troubled history. The original church was destroyed in 1241 and a new church, part of Béla IV's fortified city, was built from 1255 to 1269. Much of this Gothic building remains, but it was Mátyás Corvinus, the church's namesake, who expanded it in the 15th century. The final phase of restoration took place in 1873–96, when Frigyes Schulek redesigned it in the Neo-Baroque style.

2 Rose Window
The Neo-Gothic Rose Window **(left)** over the Main Portal was recreated by Schulek after he found fragments of an earlier window during the 19th-century restoration of the church. The original had been bricked up in the Baroque period.

1 Béla Tower
Named after Béla IV, the stout Béla Tower retains a number of its original Gothic features, though the spire and turrets are all reconstructions. Note how the tower is the least embellished part of the church.

3 Altar
This striking early Gothic-style altar **(right)**, in the shape of a cathedral, has a replica of the holy Hungarian crown atop a statue of the Virgin Mary. A shrine to the Madonna, it was designed by Schulek and completed in 1893.

Loreto Chapel and Baroque Madonna 4
Legend has it that in 1686, the Madonna **(right)** appeared before the Turks defending Buda Castle, who saw it as a sign of imminent defeat. Habsburg troops took the castle that very night.

NEED TO KNOW

MAP H2 ■ I, Szentháromság tér 2 ■ 06 1 488 77 16 ■ www.matyas-templom.hu

Open 9am–5pm Mon–Fri (to noon Sat), 1–5pm Sun; closed for mass and other events

Adm Ft2,200

Guided tours available

■ A programme giving times and dates of all upcoming classical concerts, during the summer, is available at the main entrance to the church.

■ Ruszwurm, one of Budapest's most historic cafés *(see p72)*, is just across the square and a short walk along Szentháromság utca.

5 Mary Portal
The finest example of Gothic stone carving in Hungary, this portal was rebuilt by Schulek in the 19th century, using surviving fragments of the original building.

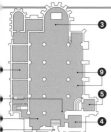

átyás Church

8 Sunday Mass
The church's two 1909 Rieger organs are the finest in Hungary, and Sunday Mass (at 10am) features the organs and the church's choir. A well-known centre of spiritual music, the church also plays host to more than 100 concerts a year.

KING MÁTYÁS
One of the greatest figures in Hungarian history, King Mátyás is often claimed by both Romanians and Serbs as being one of their own. What's certain is that Matei Corvin, as he is known in Romania, was born in Cluj-Napoca, in present-day Romania. He was the son of János Hunyadi, who in turn was the grandson of native Serbs. His family origins remain, to this day, one of the main causes of tension between Hungarian and Romanian historians *(see p14)*.

9 Stained-Glass Windows
Designed by Frigyes Schulek and painted by Károly Lotz, the three windows on the church's southern side depict the Virgin Mary's life, the family of Béla IV and the life of St Elizabeth of Árpádház, who was married at 13, widowed at 19 and died at 24.

6 Hidden Images of King Louis
Enter the church through the main portal and turn and look up to see images of King Louis the Great and his wife on the uppermost pillar beside the portal. They date from the 14th century.

7 Tomb of King Béla III and Anne de Châtillon
Schulek designed this elaborate tomb after the mortal remains of Béla III and his first wife were found during excavations at Székesfehérvár Cathedral in 1862.

10 Roof
The splendid multicoloured tiled roof **(below)** was added between 1950 and 1970. The original roof, a plain affair, burnt down after Soviet shelling during the siege of Buda in 1944–5.

TOP 10 ⭐ Hungarian State Opera

Nowhere in Budapest is the ancien regime as alive and well as at the Hungarian State Opera, architect Miklós Ybl's magnum opus. A Neo-Renaissance masterpiece built in 1884, when money was no object, its interior is a study in opulence and grandeur. A rival to any opera house in the world, its roll call of musical directors reads like a who's who of Central European music – Ferenc Erkel, Gustav Mahler and Otto Klemperer, among others.

④ Foyer Murals
Painted by Bertalan Székely and Mór Than, the foyer's sensational murals cover the entire ceiling and depict the nine Muses and other allegorical scenes.

① Façade
The passage of time has been kind to Andrássy Avenue (see p95), and the Hungarian State Opera is not as hemmed in as the city's other notable buildings. The opera features an impressive façade (above) of colonnades, balconies and loggias.

⑤ Main Stage
During the building of the Opera, the Vienna Ring Theatre was destroyed by fire. As a safety measure, an iron curtain and all-metal stage hydraulics plus a sprinkler system were installed, making the Hungarian Opera the most modern theatre in the world at that time.

② Main Entrance
Stand under the Hungarian State Opera's sublime entrance with its muralled ceilings, and you will immediately wish you were part of 19th-century Budapest society, stepping out of a horse-drawn carriage to attend a premiere.

⑥ Statues of Liszt and Erkel
The busts of Hungary's two greatest composers – Franz Liszt and Ferenc Erkel – stand guard on either side of the entrance. Both were sculpted by Alajos Stróbl, who was responsible for much of the building's interior design.

③ Foyer
The foyer (right) is a wonderful riot of murals, columns, chandeliers and gilded vaulted ceilings. Ostentation to rival Vienna was the order of the day, and Ybl did not disappoint his patrons.

8 Main Staircase

A red carpet covers the marble stairs **(left)**, which sit beneath a huge chandelier in one of the Hungarian State Opera's classic set pieces. The gilded ceiling panels contain nine paintings (by Than) of the awakening and triumph of music.

BÁNK BÁN

Hungary's most famous opera, Bánk Bán, was written by Ferenc Erkel and premiered in 1861. The story begins with Otto, brother of Queen Gertrud, who plans to seduce the wife of a faithful Hungarian viceroy, Bánk. The knight Biberach tells Bánk of Otto's evil scheme, and Bánk joins in a rebellion against the court. Rarely performed today, it was made into a film by Csaba Káel in 2001.

10 Chandelier

Above the auditorium, a fine 2,722-kg (3-ton) Mainz chandelier **(left)** illuminates a magnificent fresco by Károly Lotz of the Greek gods on Olympus. The chimney located above it facilitates ventilation.

7 Royal Box

Ybl always insisted that the Royal Box was his finest achievement. With sculptures that symbolize the four operatic voices – soprano, alto, tenor and bass – it is in the centre of a circle of three-tiered boxes.

9 Museum

The museum houses memorabilia of famous performers who have graced this stage. Sándor Svéd, a renowned Hungarian baritone who performed at New York's Metropolitan for years, features prominently.

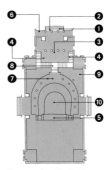

Hungarian State Opera

NEED TO KNOW

MAP M2 ■ VI, Andrássy út 22 ■ 06 1 814 71 00; Box office: 06 1 332 79 14; ■ www.opera.hu

Open Times vary, check website for details

Guided tours available

■ View the façade, the main entrance and the foyer all day, as the ticket office is open daily from 11am to 5pm. To see the rest of the building, join a guided tour.

■ The best way to see the Opera House is by watching a show. Concert tickets are usually cheaper than in Western Europe, but for lower prices, visit the Erkel Theatre, another venue of the Hungarian State Opera, at II. János Pál pápa tér 30 (06 1 332 61 50).

■ Stop at Muvész Coffee House at Andrássy út 29 for cakes.

TOP 10 ⭐ Hungarian National Museum

Since its founding in 1802, this fascinating museum has been home to Hungary's finest collection of art, artefacts and documents relating to the country's troubled history. The building is a timeless piece of Neo-Classical architecture designed by Mihály Pollack, while the impressive interior has frescoes by Károly Lotz and Mór Than.

6 Processional Crucifix

This crucifix **(above)** is from Szerecseny. A similar piece is in the St Stephen Museum in Székesfehérvár; the two are likely to have originated from the same workshop. In Hungary, many such crucifixes were found in churches destroyed during the Tatar invasion in 1241.

1 Monomachos Crown

The exquisitely crafted crown **(above)** is made of gold plaques that date from between 1042 and 1050. The gold leaf is decorated with allegories of the Great Virtues, which were popular in Byzantine art.

2 Coronation Mantle

This silk gown with the figures of Christ and the Apostles was given to a church in Székesfehérvár by St Stephen in 1031. It was later a coronation coat for Hungarian kings.

3 Funeral Crown

Found in Margaret Island's church in 1838, this golden crown dates from the 13th century and was worn by a female member of an Árpád family on her deathbed.

4 Electioneer-March in Front of the National Museum

As the title suggests, this pre-Secession painting by Franz Weiss shows the political campaigning of reformists and conservatives between 1847 and 1848, when, unlike most Western nations, Hungary was still characterized by feudalism.

7 Sabretache Plate, Galgóc

This plate is one of the finest examples of the palmette ornamental style of the Conquest period. In the shamanistic beliefs of the time, palmettes symbolized the Tree of Life.

5 Mozart's Clavichord

This travelling clavichord **(above)** was bought for the young Wolfgang Amadeus Mozart by his father, Leopold Mozart. It was used by the child prodigy to practise upon during their concert tours.

8 Diadem

Dating from the Hun period in the 5th century AD, this stunning gold diadem **(above)** is the most ancient of its kind. It was found in Csorna and is studded with 158 precious stones.

Hungarian National Museum Floorplan

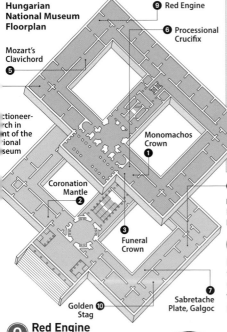

Mozart's Clavichord
5

Red Engine **9**

Processional Crucifix **6**

ctioneer-ch in nt of the ional seum

Monomachos Crown **1**

Coronation Mantle **2**

Funeral Crow **3**

Golden Stag **10**

Sabretache Plate, Galgoc **7**

Diadem **8**

Key to Floorplan
- 1st floor
- 2nd floor

10 Golden Stag

An almost flawless hand-forged figure from the 6th century BC, the Golden Stag **(below)** was part of a Scythian prince's shield.

FERENC AND ISTVÁN SZÉCHENYI

The National Museum may not have existed at all without the vast collection of art and artefacts donated in 1802 by Count Ferenc Széchényi, who also established the National Library. His equally illustrious son, Count István Széchényi, is regarded as one of the greatest Hungarians. An aristocratic poly-math, István wrote several treatises for the betterment of peasants, advocated land reform, dabbled in revolutionary politics and even paid for the country's first railway.

9 Red Engine

Painted by Sándor Bortnyik, this Cubist-style work is a fine example of activist art from the first quarter of the 20th century. Bold colours such as red and blue have been contrasted with white to highlight the sense of movement.

NEED TO KNOW

MAP M5 ■ VIII, Múzeum körút 14–16 ■ 06 1 338 21 22 ■ www.mnm.hu

Open 10am–6pm Tue–Sun

Adm Ft2,600; Ft800 for EU citizens under 26

and over 62; free for over-70s

■ The Hungarian National Museum is set on three levels. The basement has a Roman mosaic, the first floor is home to exhibits from the 5th century BC

to the Middle Ages, and the second floor houses exhibits dating from the 11th century to the present day.

■ There is a good café at the Múzeum Kávéház és Étterem *(see p93)*, next to the National Museum.

🔟⭐ Great Synagogue

Europe's largest synagogue was built in a Byzantine-Moorish style to the designs of Viennese architect Ludwig Förster between 1854 and 1859. Accommodating more than 3,000 worshippers, it also features a museum packed with historical relics and Judaic devotional items, and a moving Holocaust Memorial.

Chandeliers ③

The two Spanish-style chandeliers **(right)** above the main aisle are similar to those at the Hungarian State Opera: the design was common in concert halls throughout Europe at the time.

① Twin Towers, Onion Domes

The Great Synagogue was the first in Europe to feature 43-m- (140-ft-) high Moorish towers **(above)**, topped with Byzantine onion domes adorned with gold.

④ Organ Concerts

The original 5,000-pipe organ – installed in 1859 and played by Franz Liszt during the synagogue's dedication ceremony – was replaced with a mechanical organ in 1996. Concerts are held regularly throughout the summer.

② Upper Galleries

When built, the highly ornamented upper galleries **(above)** were designed for women who, according to tradition, had to worship separately. Today all worshippers sit downstairs.

⑤ Rose Windows

The rose window set into the façade above the main entrance is a reference to the architecture of Hungary's medieval churches.

⑥ Menorah Paving

A Menorah is depicted on the ground in front of the synagogue. Most visitors focus on the building, so it often goes unnoticed.

(8) Hungarian Jewish Museum

This museum (**above**) is home to a collection of historical Judaica from ancient Rome to the 20th century. There's also a memorial to the 600,000 Hungarian Jews killed during the Holocaust. It is dedicated to Raoul Wallenberg.

(9) The Ark

The Ark (**above**) contains a number of scrolls saved from other synagogues and hidden by Hungarian Catholic priests from the Nazis during World War II.

(7) Inscription Above the Main Entrance

Engraved in gold over the entrance is a verse in Hebrew from the book of Exodus: "And let them make me a sanctuary that I may dwell among them".

The Ten Commandments (10)

Two stone tablets (**above**) which sit atop the synagogue, resemble the shape of the building and are engraved in Hebrew with the Ten Commandments.

RAOUL WALLENBERG

Swedish diplomat Raoul Wallenberg is credited with saving as many as 100,000 Hungarian Jews during 1944–5, mainly by issuing them with Swedish travel documents. Wallenberg also negotiated directly with Major-General Gerhard Schmidthuber, head of the German forces in Hungary, to prevent the planned liquidation of the Budapest Ghetto early in January 1945. Days later, however, after the Red Army had occupied Budapest, Wallenberg was arrested as a spy by the Soviet Union and taken to Moscow's Lubianka Prison. He is believed to have died of a heart attack there in 1947. He was declared Righteous Among the Nations by the Israeli government in 1996.

A memorial to Raoul Wallenberg stands on the corner of Szilágyi Erzsébet fasor and Nagyajtai utca (Map N1).

NEED TO KNOW

MAP D4 ■ VII, Dohány utca 2 ■ 06 1 462 04 77 ■ www.jewishtourhungary.com

Open Times vary, check website for details

Adm Ft5,500

Hourly tours in several languages from 10am Sun–Fri

■ Tours of the Jewish Quarter run six times a day (Sun–Fri).

■ Kosher Deli, behind the synagogue at Síp utca 12, serves delicious kosher dishes.

The Top 10
of Everything

The thermal pool and Neo-Baroque
buildings of Széchenyi Baths

🔟 Moments in History

1 AD 409: Huns Conquer Aquincum

Established in the area that now lies on the city's northern periphery, Aquincum *(see p101)* was an important town and military garrison in the Roman province of Pannonia. It was conquered by the Huns in AD 409, and subsequently ruled by the Goths, the Longobards and the Avars.

2 AD 896: Árpád Leads the Magyars into Pannonia

Prince Árpád led the nomadic Magyars – tribes which originated in the Urals and inhabited an area east of the River Tisza – into Pannonia in AD 896. He settled first on Csepel Island, in the middle of the Danube in southern Budapest, and later in the Óbuda (meaning Ancient Buda in Hungarian).

Prince Árpád, leader of the Magyars

3 1000: Stephen I Crowned King

Stephen (István) was the first Magyar to accept Christianity and, for doing so, the pope crowned him king. He cemented the Árpád dynasty, which lasted a further 300 years.

Coronation of King Stephen I

4 1687: The Beginning of the Age of the Habsburgs

The Habsburgs became rulers of Hungary more by stealth than conquest. They completed their takeover in 1687, when the Hungarians gave up their right to elect their king, and ceded the crown to the Habsburg Empire. In one guise or another, they ruled Hungary until 1918.

5 1849: Chain Bridge Links Buda and Pest

The first permanent bridge over the Danube, the Chain Bridge was designed by Englishman William Tierney Clark, and built by a Scotsman, Adam Clark. Its completion in 1849 allowed the unification of Buda, Óbuda and Pest 24 years later.

6 1916: Charles IV Crowned Last King of Hungary

On the death of Emperor Franz József in 1916, Charles IV became king of Hungary. He abdicated in November 1918 and, despite attempting to regain the throne in 1919 after the defeat of Béla Kun's Communists, he was exiled to Madeira, Portugal, where he died in 1922.

7 1944: The Budapest Ghetto is Created

In 1944, the Nazis and their Hungarian allies, the Arrow Cross, forced over 70,000 Jews to move to the area around the Great Synagogue *(see pp36–7)*. Over 20,000 Jews died; the 50,000 that survived were liberated by the Soviet army in February 1945.

⑧ 1956: The Hungarian Uprising

Following mass anti-Soviet demonstrations in October 1956, the Hungarian Communist Party's Central Committee elected the popular politican Imre Nagy as prime minister. On 4 November, however, just 18 days after he assumed office, the Soviet army invaded Hungary and crushed the new regime. Nagy was arrested and executed in 1958.

Crowds support the proclamation of the Republic of Hungary

⑨ 1989: The People's Republic Comes to a Peaceful End

Anticipating the changes that would eventually sweep through the whole of Eastern Europe, Communist authorities in Hungary sanctioned the creation of opposition political parties in February 1989. The People's Republic of Hungary became the Republic of Hungary in October, and in March 1990, free elections were held for the first time since 1947.

⑩ 2004: Hungary Joins the European Union

After ten years of negotiations, Hungary became a full member of the European Union on 1 May 2004. The occasion was marked with days of celebrations throughout the country, and was greeted positively by most of the population. Hungary had previously become a member of NATO in 1999.

TOP 10 GREAT HUNGARIANS

1 István Széchenyi (1790–1860)
Leader of modernization and economic reforms in the 19th century, given the epithet "The Greatest Hungarian".

2 Mihály Vörösmarty (1800–55)
19th-century poet and author of the epic *The Flight of Zalán*.

3 Ferenc (Franz) Liszt (1811–86)
Hungarian composer, regarded by many as the best pianist of all time.

4 Miklós Ybl (1814–91)
Architect whose work includes the peerless Hungarian State Opera *(see pp32–3)*.

5 Sándor Petőfi (1823–49)
The recital of Petőfi's poem *Nemzeti Dal* (National Song) and "12 pont" (12 points) sparked a revolt *(see p34)* on the steps of the National Museum in 1848.

6 Béla Bartók (1881–1945)
One of the most important composers of the 20th century.

7 László Bíró (1899–1985)
Eccentric journalist who invented the world's first ballpoint pen in 1939.

8 Mária Telkes (1900–95)
A pioneer in solar energy and the inventor of a portable desalination unit that reclaims drinking water from sea water.

9 Ferenc Puskás (1927–2006)
Footballer who led the great Hungarian team of the 1950s *(see p102)*.

10 Katalin Karikó (b. 1955)
Biochemist whose research led to the development of the first set of COVID-19 vaccines.

Katalin Karikó

🔟 Places of Worship

seminal events, including the marriage of King Mátyás, and the coronations of Franz József I in 1867 and Charles IV in 1916.

3 Inner City Parish Church

Almost destroyed to make way for Elizabeth Bridge (see p46) when it was being rebuilt after World War II, the Inner City Parish Church (see p89) was miraculously saved when the builders had a last-minute change of heart. The oldest building in Pest, dating from the 14th century, it was damaged by fire in 1723 and rebuilt by György Pauer in 1725–39. Make sure to visit the elegantly vaulted Gothic chapel.

1 St Stephen's Basilica

The grandest of Budapest's many spectacular churches is fittingly named after the country's first king, St Stephen. Built in the latter part of the 19th century, it (see pp16–17) dominates the city skyline and can be seen from most parts of Budapest.

2 Mátyás Church

Mátyás Church (see pp30–31) has been bound up with Budapest history since the 13th century. It has been the stage for a number of

4 Great Synagogue

Completed in 1859, this is the largest synagogue (see pp36–7) in Europe. Its design is an eclectic mix of styles, including Byzantine twin towers, complete with onion domes, and rose windows common in Catholic churches. Inside there's a magnificent organ, which was installed in 1859. During World War II, the synagogue was used as a detention centre and also acted as the centre of the Budapest Ghetto.

Impressive nave of the Great Synagogue

Interior of the Cave Church

5 Cave Church
The remarkable Cave Church *(see p75)* was built into Gellért Hill by Pauline monks following a pilgrimage to Lourdes. It was consecrated on Whit Sunday 1926. Bricked up during the Communist period, it reopened in August 1989.

6 St Anne's Church
MAP H1 ▪ I, Batthyány tér 7 ▪ 06 1 201 63 64 ▪ Open for services only

The twin-towered parish church of Víziváros is one of the most beautiful Baroque churches in Hungary. Built between 1740 and 1805, its highlights include the painted ceiling by Gergely Vogl, the high altar and the magnificent Baroque pulpit.

7 Serbian Church
MAP L5 ▪ V, Szerb utca 2–4 ▪ Open 10am–6pm Tue–Sun

Built by Serbian settlers in 1698, this Baroque church replaced an earlier one on the same site. The church's interior is arranged according to the Greek Orthodox tradition, as the Serbs follow the Orthodox liturgy. The iconostasis that surrounds the choir gallery and divides it from the sanctuary dates from 1850.

8 Lutheran Church
MAP L3 ▪ V, Deák tér 5 ▪ Open 10am–6pm Tue–Sun ▪ eom.lutheran.hu/en

This striking church is characterized by its simplicity, in keeping with the design of most Protestant churches throughout Central Europe. Built between 1797 and 1808, it is not without charm. Superb acoustics make it a popular venue for classical and organ concerts.

9 Franciscan Church
MAP L4 ▪ V, Ferenciek tere 9 ▪ 06 1 317 33 22 ▪ Open 5:30am–noon, 4–7:45pm daily

Founded in the 13th century, the Franciscan Church – like many in Budapest – was used as a mosque during the Turkish occupation in the 16th and 17th centuries. It was rebuilt by the Franciscan Order between 1727 and 1743, and their emblem remains visible in the main portal. Numerous sculptures of Franciscan saints decorate the church's façade.

Exterior of the Capuchin Church

10 Capuchin Church
MAP H2 ▪ I, Fő utca 32 ▪ 06 1 201 47 25 ▪ Open 10:15–11:45am Tue–Fri (also open by prior arrangement)

Just a short walk along Fő utca from St Anne's Church lies the charming Capuchin Church, a 19th-century replica of an earlier building. The first church on the site was founded in the 14th century, but was converted into a mosque during the Turkish occupation and almost completely destroyed in 1686. Of the few original features to remain is the doorway on the southern façade.

🔟 **Museums and Galleries**

The Hungarian Jewish Museum

1 Hungarian Jewish Museum

MAP M4 ▪ VII, Dohány utca 2
▪ 06 1 342 89 49 ▪ Opening times
vary, check website ▪ Closed Jewish
hols ▪ Adm ▪ www.milev.hu

Budapest's proud Jewish community
is based around the Great Synagogue
(see pp36–7), and the Hungarian
Jewish Museum can be found in a
wing to the left of the Synagogue's
main entrance. Established in 1931,
it is home to thousands of historic
relics and devotional items. There is
also a room devoted to the Holocaust
and, in the courtyard, a memorial to
the 600,000 Hungarian Jews who
were killed by the Nazis.

2 Museum of Fine Arts

Housed in a Neo-Classical building,
the Museum of Fine Arts (see p95)
has a fine collection of pieces from
all artistic eras and genres. Raphael,
Toulouse-Lautrec, Picasso and Goya
all feature, and there are also
collections of ancient Egyptian
and Greek art.

3 Museum of Military History

MAP A3 ▪ I, Tóth Árpád sétány 40
▪ 06 1 325 16 00 ▪ Open 9am–5pm
Tue–Sun ▪ Adm

Located in a wing of the former
Palatine barracks, this museum
features uniforms, flags, maps,
weapons and photographs, which
document the many battles that
have been fought in Budapest. The
museum is especially effective when
it tells the story of the 1956 National
Uprising, and of the many Hungarians
who subsequently lost their lives in
the repression that followed.

4 Ludwig Museum Budapest – Museum of Contemporary Art

MAP P2 ▪ IX, Palace of Arts,
Komor Marcell utca 1 ▪ 06 1 555
34 44 ▪ Open 10am–6pm
Tue–Sun ▪ Adm ▪ www.
ludwigmuseum.hu

If the dazzling splendour
of the Habsburg Empire
and the Secession become
too much for you, head for
this museum for a refresh-
ingly vibrant display of
modern Hungarian art.
More than 150 works
dating from 1960 onwards
document the progression
of Hungarian artists as
they attempted to break
out of Socialist Realism.
There are also a number
of works by international
contemporary artists, and
changing exhibitions.

Hungarian National Museum interior

5 Hungarian National Museum

Founded on the personal collection of philanthropist Count Ferenc Széchenyi, the National Museum *(see pp34–5)* has been home to a stunning array of Hungarian artifacts since 1802, and the building is a masterpiece in its own right.

6 Hospital in the Rock

Between 1944 and1945, the network of natural caves and cellars under Buda Castle were used as an emergency military hospital and air raid shelter, providing treatment and refuge for thousands of people during the siege of Budapest. During the revolution in 1956 it was again used as a hospital. This very unique exhibition *(see p104)* offers an insight into Budapest's history. Visitors can now tour the operating rooms and wards peopled by wax figures.

7 Vasarely Museum
MAP P1 ■ III, Szentlélek tér 6 ■ 06 1 388 75 51 ■ Open 10am–6pm Fri–Sun ■ www.vasarely.hu

Born Győző Vásárhelyi, Victor Vasarely was the founder of the Op Art movement in Paris in the 1930s. This museum, based in Zichy Palace *(see p51)*, is dedicated to his life and work, and also hosts temporary 20th-century art exhibitions.

8 House of Terror Museum

This thought-provoking museum *(see p97)* tells the harrowing story of state terror carried out by both Hungary's Fascist and Communist dictatorships. Among the exhibits are grim reconstructions of prison cells and torture chambers. It also serves as a memorial to the thousands of people killed by the country's totalitarian regimes.

9 Castle Museum

Set in the labyrinthine rooms of the castle, the layout of this museum *(see p69)* can be tricky to navigate. Do persevere, as it gives fascinating insights into the history of of the city. Its real strength is in covering the story of the castle itself, starting with the ruins of the medieval castle in the Palace basement.

10 Hungarian National Gallery

Over 10,000 exhibits make the Hungarian National Gallery's collection one of the greatest in the world *(see pp26–9)*. Spread across much of the Royal Palace, almost every significant Hungarian work of art from medieval times to the present day is displayed here.

Exhibits at Hungarian National Gallery

⑩ Danube Sights

The façade of the Hungarian Parliament, seen from the Danube

① Hungarian Parliament

The city's number one sight looks better from the water or from the opposite bank of the Danube than from anywhere else. The splendour of its design – based on Britain's Houses of Parliament – is only enhanced by the river's soothing effect *(see pp12–15)*.

② River Cruises

MAP K4 ▪ Mahart Passnave: V, Vigadó tér, Dock 5–6; 06 1 484 40 13; www.mahartpassnave.hu

Several companies run tours along the Danube in the summer months. The vast majority of tours depart from Vigadó Square. Mahart Passnave operates evening cruises – including drinks and dinner – to Vienna. There are also hydrofoil services to Vienna twice a week, running from the end of April to the end of September.

③ Elizabeth Bridge

MAP K5

Hailed the longest suspension bridge in the world when completed in 1903, Elizabeth Bridge (Erzsébet híd) had to be completely rebuilt after World War II, and did not reopen until 1963. Great care had to be taken on the Pest side to ensure that the Inner City Parish Church *(see p89)* was not damaged during rebuilding; indeed at one stage the church's continued existence was

threatened, with the bridge-builders and the Communist authorities wanting to demolish it. A compromise was reached, however, and today the roadway passes just inches from the church's walls.

Shoes on the Danube

④ Shoes on the Danube

MAP J2

This moving memorial was created by sculptors Gyula Pauer and Can Togay in 2005, and comprises 60 pairs of iron shoes lined up at the edge of the Pest embankment, just south of the Hungarian Parliament building. The site had been used as a place of execution by fascist Arrow Cross militiamen, who shot hundreds of Jews here in 1944–5.

⑤ Margaret Island

Budapest's oasis and a great place to spend summer afternoons, Margaret Island *(see pp22–3)* was in fact three separate islands until they were joined together by ground-breaking embankment work in the latter part of the 19th century.

⑥ Margaret Bridge
MAP B2

The gateway to Margaret Island (Margit híd) was built by a Frenchman, Ernest Gouin, from 1872 to 1876, and is distinguished by its unusual chevron shape. The approach road to the island, however, wasn't added until the 1890s.

⑦ Liberty Bridge

Legendary Hungarian *turul* birds sit atop the Modernist girders of Liberty Bridge (Szabadság híd). First built in 1894–99 *(see p78)*, it was destroyed by the Nazis during World War II – this is an exact replica of the original. It was earlier known as Emperor Franz József Bridge, but the Communists opted for a less imperial name.

⑧ Castle Hill Funicular
MAP H3 ▪ I, Buda Castle, Clark Ádam tér ▪ Open 7:30am–10pm ▪ Closed 1st and 3rd Mon of every month ▪ Adm ▪ www.bkv.hu

Kids of all ages love to ride up and down the archaic funicular. The journey is short, the cabins tiny, but the views of the Danube below are superb. Also, on a chilly or rainy day, it beats walking up to the castle.

⑨ Embankment Walk
MAP B3, B4, C5 ▪ Columbus: V, Vigadó tér, Port 4; 06 1 266 90 13; open noon–midnight daily ▪ Spoon Café & Lounge: V, Vigadó tér, Port 3; 06 1 411 09 33; open noon–midnight daily; spoonboat.hu

This walk extends along most of the Pest embankment, from Liberty Bridge to Margaret Island and beyond. Several boats moored on the various quays have cafés aboard, including Columbus and Spoon.

⑩ Chain Bridge
MAP J3

Completed in 1849, the Chain Bridge (Széchenyi Lánchíd) was the first permanent crossing between Buda and Pest. On either side of the bridge are two huge towers that support the mammoth chains from which the bridge takes its name. The towers are superbly lit at night, which makes the bridge one of the city's most photographed sights. In summer, the bridge closes at weekends to host a cultural festival.

The Chain Bridge, linking Buda and Pest

🔟 Baths and Swimming Pools

1 Gellért Hotel and Baths Complex

Of all Budapest's many baths, this is perhaps the finest (see pp20–21), so it is fortunate that it is open to non-residents every day of the year. The outdoor pools feature one of the world's first artificial wave machines.

2 Lukács Baths

MAP B2 ■ II, Frankel Leó út 25–9 ■ 06 1 326 16 95 ■ Open 6am–10pm daily ■ Adm ■ www.budapestspas.hu

Opened in 1894, the Neo-Classical Lukács Baths offer three outdoor swimming pools, plus three indoor thermal pools, along with Kneipp baths, a fitness room, sauna and mud treatments.

3 Dagály Medicinal Baths and Strand

MAP P1 ■ XIII, Népfürdő út 36 ■ 0630 160 01 50 ■ Open 6am–7pm daily ■ Adm

Some way from the city centre, the Dagály Strand is Budapest's largest pool complex, comprising 10 pools, including children's pools, plus a hydrotherapy and fitness centre.

4 Széchenyi Baths

Set in a building designed by Győző Czigler in City Park, the Széchenyi Baths (see p95) offer a range of thermal water treatments. The complex has a number of outdoor and indoor pools.

Serene interior of Magnolia Day Spa

5 Magnolia Day Spa

MAP J2 ■ V, Zoltán útca 3 ■ 06 1 269 06 10 ■ Open noon–8pm Wed–Fri, 10am–8pm Sat & Sun ■ www.mag noliadayspa.hu

This spa in the heart of Budapest uses only natural ingredients and offers over 100 types of massages, plus body and facial treatments, manicures and pedicures.

6 Hajós Alfréd National Swimming Pool

MAP B1 ■ XIII, Margaret Island ■ 06 1 450 42 00 ■ Open 6am–7pm daily ■ Adm ■ www.mnsk.hu

Designed by architect and sportsman Alfréd Hajós, who represented Hungary at the 1896 Olympic Games in swimming and football, the three sports pools (including an Olympic-size one) are still used by the national swimming team for training.

Outdoor pools at Széchenyi Baths

7 Palatinus Strand
MAP P1 ■ XIII, Margaret Island
■ 06 1 340 45 00 ■ Open 9am–7pm
daily; air pools open only in summer;
wellness facility open all year round
■ Adm ■ http://en.palatinusstrand.hu
Budapest's most popular swimming
complex has water slides, pools and
hot springs, all set amidst the peace
of Margaret Island.

8 Veli Bej Bath
MAP B2 ■ II, Árpád Fejedelem
útja 7 ■ 06 1 438 88 87 ■ Open 6am–
noon & 3–9pm daily ■ Adm; minimum
age 14 ■ www.irgalmasrend.hu
Originally built in 1574, this Turkish
bath has five thermal pools of varying
temperatures, a Jacuzzi, two steam
cabins, saunas, massage showers,
a Kneipp bath, a swimming pool
and a variety of wellness services.

The historic Rudas Baths

9 Rudas Baths
MAP K5 ■ I, Döbrentei tér 9
■ Spa baths: 6am–8pm daily; night
baths: 10pm–3am Fri & Sat; Turkish
baths (men only): 6am–8pm Mon,
Wed & Thu, 6am–12:45pm Fri; Turkish
baths (women only): 6am–8pm Tue;
Turkish baths (mixed bathing): 1–8pm
Fri, 6am–8pm Sat & Sun ■ Adm
■ www.budapestspas.hu
The Rudas Baths (see p78), built by the
Turks in the 16th century, are among
the oldest in the city. There are six
steam pools and a swimming pool.

10 Ensana Thermal Margaret Island
Budapest's most exclusive baths are
those at the opulent Ensana Thermal
Margaret Island (see p23).

TOP 10 BATH TIPS

Relaxing shoulder massage

1 Massage
Almost all baths and pools offer various
forms of massage (for an extra cost)
that are often relaxing and refreshing.

2 Payment
The price list, posted in Hungarian,
German and English at the entrance
to all the baths, usually runs to several
pages. The entrance fee is charged
according to the service you demand
and is valid for a day. Last admission
is 1 hour before closing time.

3 Towels
Bring your own towel, or hire one for
a small fee and an additional deposit.

4 Bathrobes
In baths where men and women bathe
separately (such as the Rudas Baths),
you will be handed a small sheet.

5 Lockers
Most baths have secure lockers where
you can leave valuables for a small fee.

6 Water Temperature
All baths display the temperature
of the water by the side of the pool.

7 Steam Rooms
Entrance to the steam room – where
there is one – is usually included in
the standard entrance fee.

8 Etiquette
Most of the thermal baths are unisex.
In single-sex baths and facilities
swimming costumes are optional.

9 Wave Pools
Gellért, Dagály and Palatinus Strand
all have artificial wave machines.

10 Family Bathing
Children are welcome in most of the
city's baths, but the thermal baths
are only for over-14s.

🔟 Off the Beaten Track

1 Kiscelli Museum
MAP P1 ▪ III, Kiscelli utca 108 ▪ 06 1 250 03 04 ▪ Open 10am–6pm Tue–Sun ▪ Adm ▪ www.kiscelli muzeum.hu

While the exhibitions at the Kiscelli Museum offer a fascinating look at the history of Budapest over the past three centuries, the main attraction here is the stunning building itself, an elegant 18th-century former monastery in a mix of architectural styles, perched on a wooded hill.

2 People's Park
Locals will say that City Park, or Városliget, is for tourists, while real Budapesters head for Népliget, or People's Park (see p102). The park is home to the city's planetarium which is currently under renovation. Though it's hard to imagine today, its paths formed the circuit for the Hungarian Grand Prix in 1936.

3 Lukács Baths
Not as celebrated as some of the better known Budapest bath houses, the Lukács Baths (see p48) offer a local experience. The ticketing system is complicated and you may need an English-speaking local to help, but it all adds to the impression that you are far from the tourist crowds here. Prices are much lower, too.

Fresh produce stalls at Lehel Market

4 Lehel Market
MAP D2 ▪ XIII, Lehel tér ▪ Open daily

A bit of an eyesore from the outside, this is nevertheless the Budapest market to visit if you want a local shopping experience. Keep an eye open for farmers selling fresh produce direct from their own plots, as well as a huge range of delicious homemade cheeses.

5 Tomb of Gül Baba
MAP B2 ▪ II, Mecset utca 14 ▪ 06 1 237 44 00 ▪ Open 10am–6pm daily ▪ Adm

A 400-year-old dome covers the tomb of Gül Baba, a Muslim dervish who died in 1541, just after the fall of Buda. He was well-respected by the people of Hungary. Surrounded by a rose garden, the tomb is engraved with golden citations from the Qur'an.

6 Mikszáth Kálmán Square and Budapest VIII
MAP D5 ▪ VIII, Mikszáth Kálmán tér

Even just a decade ago this square, along with much of the historic Budapest VIII district, was something

of a no-go area for tourists. However, private investment in its handsome yet long-neglected buildings has rejuvenated the whole area, and it now has an appealing bohemian vibe, with funky shops, chic galleries, and a buzzing nightclub scene. In summer, the square is a great place to people-watch, with locals and visitors enjoying the café terraces.

 Fő Square, Óbuda
MAP P1

The focus of Fő Square, in the suburb of Óbuda, is the Zichy Palace, a must-see for those in the know, and home to museums dedicated to the avant-garde works of Vasarely (see p45) and Kassák (see p104). The Neo-Baroque Fő Square Palace opposite is perhaps even more impressive, while just north of the square on Laktanya utca is a group of statues, *Women with Umbrellas*, by contemporary sculptor Imre Varga.

 Pálvölgy Caves

These caves are less well-known than the more accessible Szemlő-hegy Caves (see p101). The most spectacular sights at Pálvölgy can be reached only via steep ladders and by navigating tricky natural rock formations as part of a 3-hour tour with an experienced guide (see p103).

9 Holocaust Memorial Center

The interactive multimedia exhibition at this centre (see p91) tells the story of Hungary's Jewish and Roma communities during the Holocaust. Exhibits here include newsreels, photographs and personal and religious items. The centre also contains the restored 1924 Páva Street Synagogue, which houses a memorial wall engraved with the names of those who lost their lives during the Holocaust.

Interior of Páva Street Synagogue

10 Aquincum

It's a pity that Aquincum (see p101) – one of the largest Roman sites in central Europe – is not more popular with visitors to Budapest. Wandering its ancient streets is a joy, not least early in the morning, when you may have the place to yourself.

Ruined buildings of the ancient Roman city of Aquincum

🔟 Children's Attractions

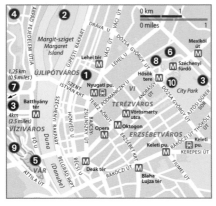

2 Palatinus Strand

Margaret Island is home to Palatinus Strand (see p49), Budapest's most popular swimming pool and thermal bath complex. Slides and a variety of children's pools make it a popular choice for families.

3 Cogwheel Railway and Children's Railway

Children's Railway: MAP N1–2; XII, Golfpálya út; 06 1 397 53 92; open 9am–4pm daily (last trains vary); adm; www.gyermekvasut.hu

■ **Cogwheel Railway:** MAP N1–2; II, Városmajor station, Szilágyi Erzsébet fasor 16; 06 1 355 41 67; open 5am–11:45pm daily; adm; www.bkk.hu

Children aged 9 to 14 operate a narrow-gauge railway that passes through the Buda Hills (see p101) from Széchenyi Hill to Hűvös Valley. The only adults on board are the engineers. To get to the train, take the cogwheel railway up from Városmajor. This track is 3,730 m (12,240 ft) long and climbs to 315 m (1,035 ft).

1 Flipper Museum

MAP C2 ■ VIII, Radnóti Miklós utca 18 ■ Open 4–11pm Wed–Fri, 2–11pm Sat, 10am–10pm Sun ■ Adm ■ www.flippermuzeum.hu

This wacky museum is home to a treasure-trove of over 130 pinball machines, from late 19th century examples to state-of-the-art pinball tables from the 21st century. Almost all of them can be played, and there is also a selection of old video games, and foosball and air hockey tables, too.

4 Csopa – Center of Scientific Wonders

MAP E3 ■ III, Bécsi út 38–44 ■ Open 10am–7pm daily ■ Adm ■ www.csopa.hu

Hungary's first hands-on science exhibition, Csopa offers a playful learning experience for all ages. Experience the world of physics here with over 100 live science shows and exhibits. There is also a family programme.

5 Castle Hill Funicular

Children adore riding in the front cabin of the Castle Hill funicular (see p47). The journey takes just three minutes or so, but the views of the Danube as you go up to the castle are magnificent, and the two replica 1870 cars, Margit and Gellért are charming.

Pinball machines at Flipper Museum

Acrobats at Capital Circus

aquarium, an impressive aviary and a superb reptile house. The staff speak several languages and are good at educating children about the animals.

9 Labyrinth
MAP G2, G3 ■ I, Úri utca 9 ■ 06 1 212 02 07 ■ Open 10am–7pm daily ■ Adm ■ www.labirintus.eu

Older children will love exploring this underground maze of tunnels and chambers. It is thought that the caves, which are around 15 m (49 ft) below ground level, were formed by hot springs about half a million years ago. They were a refuge for hunters and gatherers from around 10000 BC, and even served as a bomb shelter during World War II. A special exhibition on the infamous prisoner Vlad Tepes, also known as Dracula, includes a torture chamber and mannequins of his victims.

6 Capital Circus
MAP E2 ■ XIV, City Park (Városliget), Állatkerti körút 12/a ■ 06 1 343 83 00 ■ Daily performances: 3pm Wed–Sat (also 7pm Sat) ■ Adm ■ www.fnc.hu

This permanent circus offers plenty of fun for the entire family. The programme varies, but the focus is on remarkable feats of acrobatics, often from well-known international acts. Light and water shows, high-wire acts and clowns often feature. In summer, the circus hosts the International Circus Festival. Shows are over two hours long, so may tire small children.

7 Memento Park
Young history buffs will enjoy this impressive open-air museum (see p102), which combines gargantuan statues of the likes of Vladimir Lenin and Karl Marx with a hands-on, interactive exhibition dedicated to Hungary's Communist past. There's also the chance to take a ride in a Trabant, an iconic Communist-era car, and shop for Soviet-style memorabilia in the gift shop.

8 Budapest Zoo
Budapest's zoo (see p97) is large, well funded and one of the best in the region. It has a large

City Park Boating Lake

10 Open-Air Skating Rink and Boating Lake
MAP E2 ■ City Park (Városliget), Budapest XIV ■ Boating Lake: Olof Palme sétány 5; 0620 261 52 09; open 10am–10pm; adm ■ Skating Rink: 06 1 363 26 73; open late Oct–early Mar; timings vary; adm; www.mujegpalya.hu

In winter, City Park Lake turns into a superb skating rink, where people skate to classical music. During the summer, boats replace the skaters, as families row their craft around the lake. Skates and boats can both be hired at the jetty near the pavilion. There is also a visitors' centre.

🔟 Restaurants

Regal interiors of the Onyx Restaurant

1 Onyx Restaurant

Connected to the legendary Gerbeaud Cukrászda *(see p57)*, Onyx *(see p85)* is the first Hungarian restaurant to be awarded two Michelin stars. It offers excellent traditional gourmet cuisine and has been known to receive plaudits for its exquisite plates of food, such as the delicious blanquette of veal with langoustine.

2 Kacsa Vendéglő

Kacsa means "duck" in Hungarian, so it's easy to guess what dominates the menu here *(see p73)*. Duck is served in many inventive and delicious guises. There is a great deal more than duck on offer, however, and the wine list is simply superb.

3 Arany Kaviár

Just north of the Castle District, this gorgeous little restaurant *(see p73)* serves an adventurous melange of local and Russian food. Some of the traditional dishes include *pelmenyi* (Russian ravioli). Hungarian and Siberian cavier is a speciality. Every dish is a work of art, and can be accompanied by carefully chosen wines or one of a number of exclusive vodkas. The charming staff will help you make sense of the menu.

4 Costes

Local gourmets swear by this sleek, contemporary restaurant *(see p93)*, which was the first in Budapest to receive a Michelin star. Visitors will be treated to an unforgettable array of colour, flavour and texture combinations here.

5 Nobu

This global restaurant's first venue in Central Europe is located here. The food at Nobu *(see p93)* is unquestionably stunning. The elite gather here to enjoy Japanese cuisine, where traditional techniques are redefined through South American flavours. There is a wide selection of cocktails and the sushi bar should not be missed.

6 Comme Chez Soi

Despite the French name, this place *(see p93)* serves fine Italian food, including some of the best seafood dishes in the city. Visitors are treated to a fantastic culinary experience as they can watch while the dishes are being freshly prepared at the open kitchen behind the bar.

7 DNB Restaurant

The flagship eatery *(see p93)* at the landmark Budapest Marriott is a stunning farm-to-table restaurant that makes wonderful use of seasonal and locally sourced ingredients. Try the pan-fried trout with pickled garlic or the roasted beetroot salad. The restaurant offers impressive views of the Danube and Buda Castle.

8 Búsuló Juhász Étterem

The views from Búsuló Juhász *(see p79)*, perfectly located on the slopes of Gellért Hill, are outstanding. This traditional restaurant offers a seasonal menu, and is worth visiting as much for the views as the food. It is great spot to enjoy a cup of coffee and cake.

9 Alabárdos Étterem

This is about the only place *(see p73)* to come for Hungarian and Transylvanian food as it used to be cooked. From the goose-liver terrine to the delicious chicken paprika with curd strudel, everything on the menu is wonderfully traditional. Prices are high but the food is worth every forint.

Alabárdos Étterem

10 Kollázs

The Gresham Palace Hotel *(see p83)* has a long and illustrious history of fine dining, and its latest flagship restaurant is the best yet. First-class food is served in a spectacular Secession-style brasserie and bar. Dishes include snacks such as goose crackling and beef confit burgers. In summer, diners can sit on a grand terrace overlooking the Danube and the Chain Bridge.

TOP 10 HUNGARIAN DISHES

Töltött paprika **(stuffed pepper)**

1 Töltött paprika
Peppers stuffed with rice and mince and served in a tomato sauce – another Transylvanian favourite.

2 Kolbász
Sausages of all types. The classic Hungarian sausage is usually very spicy.

3 Bakonyi sertésborda
Pork chop served in a creamy mushroom sauce.

4 Bélszínszelet Budapest módra
Classic Budapest beef and paprika dish, though the beef needs to be of very high quality to get the best taste.

5 Marhapörkölt tarhonyával
Traditional Hungarian beef goulash in a hot, paprika sauce, often accompanied by soft noodles.

6 Brassói aprópecsenye
Pork stew, strongly seasoned with garlic and paprika and accompanied by fried potatoes.

7 Borjúbélszín Gundel módra
Medallions of veal cooked in a rich mushroom sauce.

8 Erdélyi fatányéros
Popular Transylvanian mixed grill of pork and beef, lavishly garnished with pickles, peppers and chips. Presented on a wooden platter, each portion is intended to serve two people.

9 Libamáj zsírjában
Goose liver, fried in its own fat, is a Hungarian speciality and is considered a great delicacy.

10 Halászlé
Hungarians do not cook much fish, but this carp soup, seasoned with paprika, is popular in winter.

10 Cafés, Pubs and Bars

1 Tóth Kocsma
Despite being close to the main sights, this place *(see p84)* has the look and feel of a classic local Budapest pub. Well-priced drinks, including an extensive homemade cider menu, good bar food and pavement tables in nice weather. It's small, so be prepared to stand.

2 Szimpla Kert
This is the biggest of the seventh district's ruin pubs *(see p92)* and one of the most renowned. There is an abundance of nooks and crannies inside the building, while the outdoor area offers ample seating, as well as movies during the summer. Szimpla also hosts a series of summertime concerts featuring jazz, rock, blues and more, all of which are free.

Hip ruined-garden bar Szimpla Kert

3 Blue Bird Café
MAP M3 ■ VII, Dob utca 16 ■ 06 208 05 80 ■ **Open** 9am–10pm daily

Quirky design, award-winning coffee, big American-style breakfasts and huge slices of homemade cake make this just about the most popular café in town. It's also one of the most colourful: a riot of blue and gold. The Blue Bird also boasts a lovely interior courtyard, which makes for a blissfully cool escape from the summer heat. Pets allowed.

Hungarian wine bar Doblo

4 Doblo
There's exposed brickwork inside and out at this charming little bar *(see p92)*, which serves one of the city's largest selections of Hungarian wines, almost all of which are available by the glass. The emphasis is naturally on local wines, but you can select from an extensive international list. The knowledgeable staff are happy to make suggestions. Even the bar snacks menu has suggestions for the perfect accompanying wine.

5 Ötkert
Budapest's ruin pubs are legendary, but this place *(see p84)* gives the concept an upmarket makeover. Located in the heart of the city centre, Ötkert serves great light meals and cocktails. It becomes an informal club complete with DJs as the night wears on.

6 AlterEgo
Housed in an underground cellar, this friendly spot *(see p84)* is Budapest's top LGBTQ+ venue. Well-known for its eclectic mix of music and fun themed parties, AlterEgo also hosts popular live drag shows every Saturday night, featuring dance, stand-up and lip-syncing performances. The drinks are well priced for such a central location.

7 Boutiq'Bar

Outside of the smart hotels, downtown Pest used to have a shortage of good cocktail bars, but that is no longer the case. The team of dedicated young mixologists here *(see p84)* are adept at creating both classic and innovative cocktails. Prices are not cheap, but the quality of the drinks is superb, and the service is impeccable.

8 Café Vian

Even with big-brand coffee houses opening all over Budapest, Café Vian *(see p98)* continues to be busy both day and night. It is warm and inviting, contemporary yet traditional, and the coffee and food are fantastic.

Gerbeaud Cukrászda cakes

9 Gerbeaud Cukrászda (Café Gerbeaud)

Possibly Budapest's most famous and elegant café *(see p92)*, Gerbeaud Cukrászda is a real treat for coffee- and dessert-lovers, as well as for historians. It is worth stopping here simply to admire the brass cash register and the saloons complete with old chandeliers.

10 New York Café és Étterem

This lavish coffee house and restaurant *(see p98)* inside the New York Palace (now home to a hotel, *see p114)* has a fascinating history. Its richly frescoed ceilings and little gold chairs belie the fact that it was once a hangout for impoverished writers. The food is excellent, but portions can be small.

TOP 10 HUNGARIAN DRINKS

1 Pálinka
The Hungarian word for fruit brandy, Pálinka is distilled from fruits grown in the orchards situated on the Great Hungarian Plain.

2 Unicum
Originally prescribed as a remedy for the king by the court physician Dr Zwack, this liqueur is made with more than 40 herbs.

3 Pezsgő
Quality sparkling wine that enjoys a good reputation in Hungary.

4 Fröccs
A refreshing fizzy drink to have in hot summer, made by mixing wine with *szódavíz* (carbonated water).

5 Szódavíz
Invented by Hungarian scientist Ányos Jedlik, szódavíz is a true national drink, available at several pubs. It costs less than bottled mineral water.

6 Bikavér
Known as Bull's Blood, this dry red wine blend is produced from grapes ranging from garnet red to deep ruby.

7 Sör
Some of the best known Hungarian Sör (beer) brands are Dreher, Soproni and Borsodi.

8 Puszta koktél
Traditional cocktail of Hungary, Puszta koktél is made of Tokaji szamorodni wine, apricot brandy, Mecsek liqueur and lemon-oil or sour cherry.

9 Szörp
A homemade local fruit and herb syrup, which is used to make drinks in some bars.

10 Tokaji aszú
Best known dessert wine, made in the Tokaj wine region.

White wine from the Tokaj region

🔟 Shops and Markets

WestEnd City Center

1 WestEnd City Center
MAP C2 ▪ VI, Váci út 1–3 ▪ 06 1 238 77 77 ▪ Open 8am–10pm daily ▪ www.westend.hu

This vast, three-level complex of more than 400 shops is next to Nyugati Railway Station. All your favourite brands and stores can be found here, though don't expect bargains, as prices are often higher than at home. Don't miss the rooftop garden. Some community events also take place here.

2 Palais Herend
MAP K3 ▪ V, József nádor tér 10-11 ▪ 20 241 57 36 ▪ Open 10am–6pm Mon–Fri, 10am–2pm Sat ▪ www.herend.com

As much a museum as it is a shop, Palais is an authorized retailer of Hungary's finest porcelain, known as Herend. The Herend factory, to the west of the city, has been making exquisite porcelain for generations. Most pieces at Apponyi command high prices, and everything is housed in large, priceless wooden cabinets beneath a splendid wooden ceiling.

3 Fashion Streets
MAP K3 ▪ Deák Ferenc utca ▪ MAP L2–L3 ▪ Andrássy út

Classy fashion stores and cafés dominate two of the city's most elegant shopping streets. Deák Ferenc utca (also called Fashion Street), which runs towards Váci Street, features brands such as Hugo Boss and Tommy Hilfiger. More glamorous options line the elegant Andrássy Avenue (see p95), including Louis Vuitton and Gucci.

4 Allee
XI, Október Huszonharmadika utca 8–10 ▪ 06 1 372 72 08 ▪ Open 9am–10pm Mon–Sat (to 8pm Sun) ▪ allee.hu

Located on the Buda side of the Danube river, Allee is a modern, pet-friendly shopping mall where visitors can easily find almost anything ranging from clothing to electronics to a number of restaurants and cafés. It is popular with both locals and visitors. Many large stores are clustered here and it is easily accessible from the city centre by public transport.

Shoppers at Central Market Hall

⑤ Central Market Hall
MAP M6 ■ V, Vámház körút 1–3 ■ Open 6am–5pm Mon (to 6pm Tue–Fri, to 3pm Sat & Sun) ■ www.piaconline.hu

Budapest's main produce market is great for local delicacies. Impeccably clean, it has numerous stalls selling meat, salami, fruit and vegetables. The upper floor has several street food stalls, restaurants and souvenir shops.

⑥ Polgár Galéria
MAP M4 ■ V, Kossuth Lajos utca 3 ■ 06 1 318 69 54 ■ Open 10am–5pm Mon–Fri, 10am–12:30pm Sat ■ www.polgar-galeria.hu

A sensational art and antiques gallery, where you can purchase works by classical and contemporary Hungarian artists. You will also find rare antiques, including imperial Habsburg furniture. The gallery even looks after all onward shipping and related paperwork.

⑦ Rózsavölgyi Szalon Arts & Café
MAP L4 ■ Szervita tér 5 ■ 06 1 318 35 00 ■ Open 10am–8pm Mon–Sat ■ www.szalon.rozsavolgyi.hu

Rózsavölgyi is a treasure-trove for music lovers. Opened in 1912, this store specializes in sheet music and records. Musical instruments are sold as well. It is also a venue for theatrical and musical performances and literary and fine arts events, which you can enjoy along with a cup of coffee or a light meal.

⑧ BÁV Jewellery (Rubin Ékszerbolt)
BÁV Jewellery: MAP L4; V, Párizsi utca 2; 06 1 318 62 17 ■ BÁV: MAP K3; V, Bécsi utca 1; 06 1 429 30 20 ■ Open (both shops) 10am–6pm Mon–Sat ■ www.bav.hu

A collection of fine antique watches and jewellery from one of Hungary's best-known auction houses. There are several other BÁV shops across the city, with different specializations.

⑨ Memories of Hungary
MAP L3 ■ V, Hercegprímás út 8 ■ 06 1 780 58 44 ■ Open 10am–10pm daily ■ www.memoriesofhungary.hu

Located on the edge of St Stephen's Square, next door to the Basilica, Memories of Hungary sells traditional products made by local craftspersons and artists. Pick up a souvenir from their wide range of fabrics, porcelain, ceramics, toys, food items, jewellery and Rubik's Cubes®.

Ceramics at Memories of Hungary

⑩ WAMP - Design in the City
MAP C4 ■ V, Erzsébet tér ■ MAP A2 ■ II, Kis Rókus u. (Millenáris Park) ■ www.wamp.hu

Held occassionally on weekends in two locations, the WAMP design fair provides young Hungarian designers an opportunity to sell their handmade items including textiles, jewellery, and kitchenware. There are also stalls selling homemade delicacies.

Visitors shopping at WAMP

🔟 Budapest for Free

The Pest embankment

1 Pest Embankment

A walk along the Danube embankment from the Elizabeth Bridge to Parliament *(see pp46–7)* is an eye-opening trip through various eras of Hungarian history and architecture, all overseen by the Royal Palace on the opposite bank. Look out for street artists and musicians in summer, and pause to contemplate the moving Shoes on the Danube memorial.

2 St Stephen's Basilica

You will need to pay a small fee to view the treasury or climb to the dome, but the main attractions of Budapest's largest church *(see pp16–17)* are free: the Main Altar, featuring a stunning marble statue of St Stephen (King István); the Gyula Benczúr portrait of István dedicating Hungary to the Virgin Mary; and the Holy Right Hand, believed to be the right forearm of István himself.

3 Museums on National Holidays

Most of Hungary's state and munici-pal museums are free on national holidays *(see p63)*. The Hungarian National Gallery *(see pp26–9)*, the National Museum *(see pp34–5)* and the Museum of Fine Arts *(see p95)* are the pick of the bunch. Note that the guided tour of Parliament *(see pp12–15)* is not free.

4 Walking Tours

Budding tour guides, and locals who simply want to share their knowledge of the city, offer a number of free, themed daily walking tours during spring and summer. The unofficial meeting point for these walks is the fountain in Vörösmarty Square: get here between 10am and 11am and you should have no problem finding one to join. Although free, your guide will appreciate a tip if you find the tour worthwhile.

5 Danube Carnival

Throughout June, the Danube Carnival takes over Vörösmarty Square, the Pest embankment and – on some weekends – the Chain Bridge. Most of the concerts, parades, street art and children's events in the festival are free.

6 Gellért Hill

Gellért Hill *(see p78)* is surprisingly steep, and climbing up to the Citadel on the top offers something of a challenge to even the fittest. Make sure to stop to admire the Gellért Monument on the way up, before heading down the other side via the unique Cave Church *(see p75)*.

7 Fishermen's Bastion

The defining view of Budapest is that offered from the turrets of the Fishermen's Bastion *(see p70)* up on Castle Hill, from where you can pick out all of the city's major landmarks. Just make sure you get here early in

Fishermen's Bastion

the morning to get the best out of the place, as the crowds can be overwhelming later on.

8 City Park

Central Budapest's largest park *(see pp94–7)* offers a wide range of free things to see and do, from admiring the Millennium Monument on Heroes' Square to enjoying a walk through its surprisingly densely forested paths. The park boasts a large number of flower beds around the central lake, a riot of colour in bloom.

Vajdahunyad Castle, City Park

9 Margaret Island

Elegant Margaret Island *(see pp22–3)*, a park since the 1860s, is where Budapest residents come to find a little peace. Walk from one length to the other, past the ruins of a 13th-century Dominican monastery, a UNESCO-protected water tower and through the lush Japanese Garden, all for free.

10 Inner City Parish Church

While the Mátyás Church across the river gets all the attention and visitors (despite the steep entrance fee), most locals will tell you that the free Inner City Parish Church *(see p89)* is even more impressive. Look out for remains of the original 15th-century frescoes, as well as the *mihrab*, a reminder of the Turkish occupation.

TOP 10 BUDGET TIPS

Hungarian wine

1 Local Hungarian beer and wine is often cheaper than imported alcohol (and often tastes much better).

2 Most restaurants in the city centre – especially those close to office buildings – offer cheap set menu deals at lunchtime.

3 Budapest's main parks, People's Park (Népliget) and City Park (Városliget), make for perfect picnic spots.

4 Look out for free concerts and street performers in Vörösmarty Square and along Váci Street.

5 Most hotels in Budapest tend to offer lower rates during the week.

6 Budapest's smarter hostels usually have private rooms with bathrooms, which are much cheaper than hotels.

7 Buy a travelcard if using public transport. These are available for one, three or seven days and make travel much cheaper *(see www.bkk.hu/en)*.

8 Do what local pensioners do and visit bath houses early in the morning to grab the lowest prices.

9 The Budapest Card offers free public transport and reduced price admission to a number of museums and other attractions *(see www.budapest-card.com/en)*.

10 The yellow licensed taxis have the same fixed fare. Make sure the price per kilometre is clearly displayed.

Licensed taxi in Budapest

🔟 Festivals and Events

Dancing and laser shows at Sziget Festival of pop and rock music

1 Budapest Spring Festival
www.btf.hu

The Budapest Spring Festival runs for two weeks in April and features world-class performers. Outstanding opera, chamber and classical music, literature and theatre take over almost every performance art venue in the city.

2 Budapest Dance Festival
www.budapesttancfesztival.hu

Paying tribute to the art of dance, and usually held during late February, this festival introduces the season's productions, features foreign companies and honours the year's best Hungarian dance artists. The host institutes are the National Dance Theatre and Hungary's cultural hub, the Palace of Arts.

3 Budapest Summer Festival
www.szabadter.hu

The Budapest Summer Festival takes place every weekend from June until August. Both international and Hungarian theatre and music shows take place in the city's parks.

4 Hungarian Grand Prix
www.hungaroring.hu

The Hungaroring circuit is 19 km (12 miles) from Budapest. The city goes into Grand Prix mode at least a week before the race (usually held in July). Tickets are expensive and best booked in advance.

5 Sziget Festival
www.sziget.hu

Central Europe's biggest pop and rock festival makes perfect use of Óbudai, an island in the middle of the Danube. The world's leading artists perform over a week in mid-August. Most revellers stay on the island the whole week, sleeping in tents.

6 Festival of Folk Arts

Each year in August, Dísz tér in the Castle District comes alive for four days of arts and crafts. Skilled craftspeople from all over Hungary flock here to display and sell their wares. There are also performances of Hungarian folk music and dance. The highlight, however, is the folk art parade that takes place on St Stephen's Day (20 August).

Parade at the Festival of Folk Arts

Jewish Summer Festival
www.zsidokulturalisfesztival.hu

This week-long celebration of Jewish culture, usually held at the end of August, features music, dance, visual arts, comedy and cabaret. For details, visit the Jewinform kiosk next to the Great Synagogue on Dohány utca (see pp36–7).

Budapest Wine Festival
www.winefestival.hu

Every September, the area around Buda Castle is filled with Hungary's finest wine merchants and artisanal food producers, who display their latest offerings. There is also a parade and a charity wine auction.

Budapest Wine Festival

Café Budapest Contemporary Arts Festival
www.cafebudapestfest.hu

"Art is communication; communication can best be learned through art". This message drives the Budapest Autumn Festival. One of Europe's leading celebrations of the contemporary arts, the festival show-cases the work of artists who have few opportunities open to them, and aims to stimulate communication among different genres.

Christmas Fair
www.budapestinfo.hu

At the end of November, Vörösmarty Square turns into a festive market for Hungarian arts, crafts and food. At 5pm daily, a new window of the Advent calendar opens on the façade of Gerbeaud Cukrászda (see p57).

TOP 10 HOLIDAYS

1 Anniversary of 1848 Revolution (15 Mar)
Hungarians pay their respects to Sándor Petőfi by re-enacting his poem at the National Museum (see pp34–5).

2 Easter (Mar/Apr)
As a largely Catholic nation, Hungarians celebrate Easter quietly at home.

3 Whit Sunday and Monday (7th Sunday and the following Monday after Easter)
This national holiday celebrates the descent of the Holy Spirit.

4 Labour Day (1 May)
Once a Communist holiday marked with processions of workers, Labour Day is still observed as a national holiday.

5 St Stephen's Day (20 Aug)
Celebrates the coronation of St Stephen (István), Hungary's patron saint, with a firework display over the Danube.

6 Republic Day (23 Oct)
A double celebration commemorates the outbreak of the 1956 revolution and the 1989 proclamation of the Republic of Hungary.

7 All Saints' Day (1 Nov)
Celebrates saints who do not have their own holy days. The preceding day, people visit cemeteries to light candles in remembrance of their lost relatives.

8 Santa Claus Day (6 Dec)
This is when children hope to find small gifts left in their polished shoes by Santa Claus (Mikulás).

9 Christmas (24–26 Dec)
The city's famed Christmas gift market takes place throughout December.

10 New Year (31 Dec)
New Year's Eve is celebrated on the streets. Vörösmarty Square usually hosts concerts and firework displays.

Christmas Nativity scene

🔟 Day Trips from Budapest

1 Visegrád
Bus from Újpest-Városkapu
■ Castle: open Mar, Apr & Oct: 9am–5pm daily; May–Sep: 9am–6pm daily; Nov: 9am–4pm daily; Dec–Feb: 10am–4pm Fri–Sun ■ Palace: open 9am–6pm Tue–Sun ■ www.visegrad.hu

The ruins of a 13th-century castle are the focal point of this palace, which stands atop a hill above the town. Visitors can explore a 20th-century reconstruction of the palace.

Royal Palace at Gödöllő

2 Gödöllő
HÉV from Örs Vezér tere
■ Grassalkovich Mansion: 0628 41 01 24; open Apr–Oct: 10am–5pm Mon–Fri, 10am–6pm Sat & Sun; Nov–Mar: 10am–4pm Mon–Fri, 10am–5pm Sat & Sun; www.kiralyikastely.hu

Open-air concerts and theatre at the 18th-century Grassalkovich Mansion at Gödöllő are highlights, but the Baroque palace and museum are also worth a look.

3 Fót
Bus from Újpest-Városkapu; train from Nyugati pu ■ Palace: www.fotikastelyetterem.hu

Fót is home to the Károlyi Palace, the birthplace of Hungary's first president, Mihály Károlyi. The Church of the Immaculate Conception, with its columned nave, is also worth a visit.

4 Kecskemét
Train from Nyugati pu ■ Town Hall: 0 676 51 22 63 ■ Cifra Palace: 0 676 48 07 76 ■ www.kecskemet.hu

Ödön Lechner's town hall (1893–6), with pink tiles and minaret-like spires, is Kecskemét's biggest draw. Another fine building is the Secession-style Cifra Palace, built as a casino in 1902.

5 Ráckeve
Bus from Népliget ■ Church: 0630 429 72 48; www.tourinform.rackeve.hu

This town's highlight is its Orthodox church, the oldest in Hungary. It was built by Serb settlers in 1487. The interior walls are covered with frescoes.

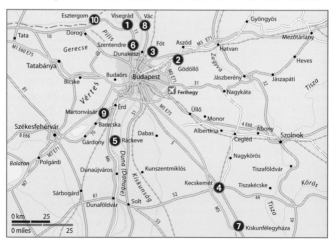

Colourful Fő Square, the main square in the riverside town of Szentendre

⑥ Szentendre
■ HÉV from Batthyány tér
■ Hungarian Open Air Museum: 0 626
50 25 00; open Mar–Nov: 9am–5pm
Tue–Sun; adm; www.skanzen.hu
■ Ferenczy Museum: open 10am–6pm
Thu–Sun; adm; www.szentendre.hu

With cobbled lanes, pastel-coloured
buildings and tall Orthodox church
spires, Szentendre is a picturesque
Hungarian town. Sights include the
Hungarian Open Air Museum, which
showcases country life from the 18th
century until World War I, and the
Ferenczy Museum's Margit Kovács
Ceramics Exhibition, which displays
the works of one of Hungary's best
ceramic artists.

⑦ Kiskunfélegyháza
■ Train from Nyugati pu ■ Park:
www.knp.hu ■ Tourist information:
06 76 56 20 39; open 8am–4pm;
www.felegyhaziturizmus.hu

Nationalist poet Sándor Petőfi (see
p41) spent a part of his childhood
in this town, and his house is now
a museum. East of town is the
Kiskunfélegyháza National Park,
a popular spot for birdwatchers.

⑧ Vác
■ Train from Nyugati pu ■ 0627
31 61 60 ■ www.tourinformvac.hu

Destroyed and rebuilt in the
17th century, this medieval town is
known for being the site of Hungary's
Arc de Triomph, built in 1764.

⑨ Martonvásár
■ Train from Déli pu
■ Brunswick Palace and Park: open
Apr–Oct: 9am–6pm daily; Nov–Mar:
10am–4pm Wed–Sun ■ www.
martonvasar.hu

Brunswick Palace at Martonvásár
is one of the best-preserved stately
homes in Hungary. The present
19th-century building, surrounded by
splendid parklands, is a copy of a late
18th-century Baroque construction.

⑩ Esztergom
■ Bus from Árpád híd; train from
Nyugati pu ■ www.esztergom.hu

The capital city from the 10th to 13th
centuries, and the site of St Stephen's
baptism and coronation, Esztergom
has played an important role in
Hungarian history. The city's vast
cathedral is the seat of Roman
Catholicism in Hungary.

The cathedral at Esztergom

Budapest
Area by Area

The Danube, the Chain Bridge
and St Stephen's Basilica at dusk

🔟 The Castle District and North Buda

A UNESCO World Heritage Site, medieval Buda grew up around its 13th-century castle, which was erected on a hill to protect it from invaders. However, that wasn't enough to deter the Turks, who attacked and then neglected Buda in the 16th century. It was the Habsburgs who finally restored the town in the 19th century, in glorious imperial style. North of the castle is Víziváros (Water Town), an area first inhabited by people too poor to live on Castle Hill. Today, it is one of the city's most exclusive residential districts.

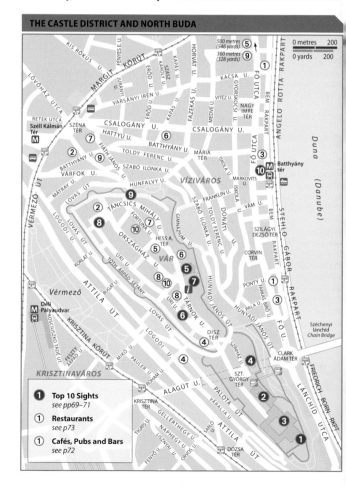

THE CASTLE DISTRICT AND NORTH BUDA

1 **Top 10 Sights**
see pp69–71

1 **Restaurants**
see p73

1 **Cafés, Pubs and Bars**
see p72

1 Castle Museum

MAP J4 ■ I, Wing E of the Royal Palace, Szent György tér 2 ■ 06 1 487 88 01 ■ Open 10am–6pm Tue–Sun ■ Adm ■ www.varmuzeum.hu

This fascinating collection of artifacts and historical documents traces the city's and the castle's history via three distinct exhibitions. The basement houses a display on the castle during the Middle Ages that includes a recreation of a vaulted chapel from the earliest 1255 structure. Gothic sculptures and armour that were unearthed while renovating the Royal Palace after World War II are also displayed. The ground floor has exhibits on the city's evolution from Roman times to the 17th century, while the first floor explores "Budapest in Modern Times". The museum is part of the wider Budapest History Museum, which also includes Aquincum *(see p101)*, and as a result locals often call it by that name.

2 Royal Palace

MAP B4

Towering above Budapest, the Royal Palace, or castle, is an amalgamation of several buildings. Most of the present Habsburg Palace was built in the 18th century during the reign of Maria Theresa, but it was preceded by a palace and two castles. The first castle was built around 1255, but was rebuilt by Mátyás I in 1458. Following damage in World War II, the palace was renovated again, with some parts, such as the dome, being entirely rebuilt. It now houses several museums, including the Castle Museum and the Hungarian National Gallery.

3 Hungarian National Gallery

It would take weeks to view all the exhibits in the Hungarian National Gallery, as there are thousands of works on display at any given time. From medieval altarpieces to striking Secession paintings, it's all here. The gallery shares its collection with the Museum of Fine Arts *(see pp26–9)*.

Hungarian National Gallery

4 Sándor Palace

MAP H3 ■ I, Szent György tér 1–3 ■ Closed to the public

The official residence of the Hungarian president can only be admired from the outside, but the superb Neo-Classical motifs and bas-reliefs by Richárd Török, Miklós Melocco and Tamás Körössényi are worth spending time over. The Palace was commissioned in 1806 by Count Vincent Sándor, and designed by Mihály Pollack and Johann Aman. It was severely damaged in 1944, and was almost entirely rebuilt after World War II.

Budapest's Royal Palace

Interior of Mátyás Church

5 Mátyás Church

Standing on the site of a 13th-century structure, Mátyás Church (see pp30–31) was rebuilt and named after King Mátyás in 1470. Through most of the Middle Ages, Hungarians were not permitted in the church; only Germans could worship here. It has witnessed several significant events, from the marriage of Mátyás to the coronations of Franz József I and Charles IV. Béla III and his wife are also buried here. When the Turks came to power in the early 1500s, they converted Mátyás Church into a mosque. According to legend, in 1686 a statue of the Madonna appeared before the Turks while they were praying. They took this as a sign of defeat and surrendered the city of Buda to the Habsburgs. The church was also the scene of fierce fighting during World War II, and was not renovated until 1968.

6 Lords' Street
MAP G2 ■ I, Úri utca

Baroque and Gothic façades give Lords' Street (Úri utca) its unique medieval character, though most of the houses were rebuilt from 1950 to 1960, after being destroyed during World War II. The street runs the full length of Castle Hill and its highlights include the Hölbling House at No. 31, with its sublime Gothic façade, the Telephony Museum at No. 49, and the bizarre but exceptional Labyrinth (see p53), whose entrance is at No. 9. The real highlight, however, is to walk from one end to the other.

7 Fishermen's Bastion
MAP H2 ■ I, Halászbástya, Szentháromság tér

From early morning until late at night, visitors head for the Fishermen's Bastion, whose turrets offer the most picturesque views of Pest, for no fee. It was built in Neo-Romanesque style by Frigyes Schulek as a monument to the Guild of Fishermen in 1895.

View from the Fishermen's Bastion

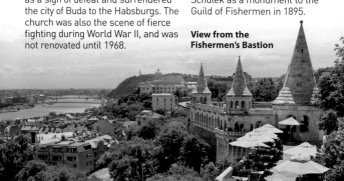

8 ### Church of St Mary Magdalene
MAP G2 ■ I, Kapisztrán tér 6

Built in the 13th century for the city's Hungarian citizens, who were forbidden from praying at Mátyás Church, this church now lies in ruins. All that remains is the tower and gate – the rest of the building was pulled down after World War II. Nevertheless, the site is enchanting, and the square in which it stands is unusually peaceful.

Vienna Gate Square

9 ### Vienna Gate Square
MAP G1 ■ I, Bécsi kapu tér

The gate you see today is, in fact, a replica of the original structure, which once led from Buda towards Vienna. It was built in 1936 to celebrate the 250th anniversary of Buda's liberation from the Turks. Quintessential Gothic and Baroque houses line the sides of the square. The huge building on the square's left-hand side is the Hungarian National Archive, a Neo-Romanesque structure famous for its multicoloured roof.

10 ### Batthyány Square
MAP H1 ■ I, Batthyány tér

In the heart of Víziváros, this square is named after Count Lajos Batthyány, the prime minister during the Hungarian Uprising of 1848–9. Though marred by traffic, the square is crammed with architectural wonders. The Hikisch House at No. 3 has bas-reliefs of the four seasons, and St Anne's Church (see p43) is a fine Baroque building. A monument to Ferenc Kölcsey, who wrote the words of the national anthem, overlooks the square.

A DAY IN THE CASTLE DISTRICT AND NORTH BUDA

▶ MORNING

There's no better way of getting up to the castle than by taking the **Funicular** (see p47) from Lánchíd utca. At the top, you can admire the stately **Sándor Palace** (see p69) from the outside, but you won't get past the smartly dressed guards unless you have business with the president. On the other side of the palace is the superb **Hungarian National Gallery** (see pp26–9). It would be easy to spend all day here, but with careful planning you should be able to see the highlights within an hour or so. Then stroll along the castle ramparts to **Lords' Street** (Úri utca), with its charming Baroque and Gothic buildings and end with a relaxing lunch at **Budavári Rétesbvár** (see p72).

AFTERNOON

Head eastwards to the **Fishermen's Bastion** and enjoy fabulous views of the Danube and Pest on the opposite bank; don't forget your camera. Next door is the historic **Mátyás Church**. You can stock up on souvenirs at the shops on **Fortuna utca** – the Hilton Budapest hotel (see p114) has a superb souvenir shop – before following the road to the ruins of the **Church of St Mary Magdalene**. From the church, take the little Castle District bus back along Lords' Street to **Ruszwurm** (see p72) for a cake or strudel. If you are lucky, there will be a concert at Mátyás Church to enjoy as well.

See map on p68 ←

Cafés, Pubs and Bars

① Henri Belga Söröző
MAP H2 ▪ I, Bem rakpart 12
▪ Open noon–midnight ▪ www.
belgasorozo.com

This pub, located next to a restaurant of the same name, serves more than 20 types of beers.

Oscar American Cocktail Bar

② Oscar American Cocktail Bar
MAP G1 ▪ I, Ostrom utca 14 ▪ 06 70
700 02 22 ▪ Open 5pm–3am Wed–Sat
▪ www.oscarbarbudapest.hu

Visit this sophisticated, cinema-themed bar to try a fantastic range of cocktails, either shaken or stirred.

③ Angelika
MAP H1 ▪ I, Batthyány tér 7
▪ Open Apr–Oct: 9am–midnight;
Nov–Mar: 9am–11pm ▪ www.
angelikacafe.hu

This historic patisserie, housed in a former crypt of St Anne's Church (see p43), serves superb pastries.

④ Korona Kávéház
MAP H3 ▪ I, Dísz tér 16 ▪ Open
10am–6pm ▪ www.koronakavehaz.hu

A traditional café which is run by the same people that manage the Ruszwurm café.

⑤ Calgary Antik Drink Bar
MAP B2 ▪ II, Frankel Leó utca 24
▪ 06 30 847 34 72 ▪ Open 4pm–4am

A cross between an antique shop, bar and club, the Calgary attracts crowds long after most places have closed.

⑥ Faust Wine Cellar
MAP G2 ▪ 1014, Hess András
tér 1–3 ▪ 06 20 326 35 03 ▪ Open
2–8pm Thu–Mon ▪ www.gbwine.eu

Escape from the bustling city to this wine cellar in the Buda Castle District. There are wine and pálinka tastings daily, and wines can be purchased by the bottle.

⑦ Móri Borozó
MAP G1 ▪ I, Fiáth János utca
16 ▪ 06 214 92 16 ▪ Open 2–11pm
Mon–Sat

Wine straight from the barrel and drunk by the glass. There is usually a good stew cooking as well.

⑧ Budavári Rétesbvár
MAP G2 ▪ I, Balta köz 4
▪ 06 70 408 86 96 ▪ Open 8am–8pm

Traditional Hungarian café known for its mouthwatering strudel.

⑨ Café Gusto
MAP B2 ▪ I, Frankel Leó utca 12
▪ 06 316 39 70 ▪ Open 8am–11pm
Mon–Sat ▪ www.gustocafe.hu

This café serves a good range of Italian coffees, generous salads and platters, and a selection of wines and spirits.

⑩ Ruszwurm
MAP G2 ▪ I, Szentháromság
utca 7 ▪ Open summer: 10am–7pm
daily; winter: 10am–6pm daily
▪ www.ruszwurm.hu

Established in 1824, this family-run café is renowned for its delicious strudel and priceless period furniture.

Nostalgic interior of Ruszwurm

Restaurants

PRICE CATEGORIES
For a three-course meal for one, with half
a bottle of wine (or equivalent meal),
taxes and extra charges.

F under Ft5,000 **FF** Ft5,000–10,000
FFF over Ft10,000

1 Kacsa Vendéglő
MAP B3 ▪ I, Fő utca 75
▪ Open noon–midnight ▪ www.
kacsavendeglo.hu ▪ FFF

Visit this outstanding restaurant *(see
p54)* for its delectable duck dishes.
Service is ostentatious, with dishes
whipped out from under silver domes.

2 Baltazár
MAP G2 ▪ I, Országház
utca 31 ▪ 06 1 300 70 51 ▪ Open
7:30am–11:45pm daily ▪ www.
baltazarbudapest.com ▪ FF

Simple yet delicious and good value
food, including locally sourced
steaks, burgers, duck and chicken.
Grab a table on the cobbled street
outside in summer.

3 Pavillon de Paris
MAP H2 ▪ I, Fő utca 20 ▪ 0620
509 34 30 ▪ Open noon–11pm daily
▪ www.pavillondeparis.hu ▪ FF

This French restaurant has seafood
as the main speciality. It also has a
great terrace and garden.

4 Stand25
MAP G3 ▪ I, Attila út 10
▪ Open noon–4pm & 6–11pm
Mon–Sat ▪ www.stand25.hu ▪ FFF

Elegant restaurant serving contemporary Hungarian cuisine, such as
veal meatloaf with split pea puree.

5 Budavári Mátyás
MAP G2 ▪ I, Hess András tér 4
▪ 06 30 984 75 18 ▪ Open 11am–11pm
daily ▪ FFF

Locals flock to this beer bar to sit
at one of the long tables and drink,
eat and be merry. Join in and feast
on their menu of simple but delicious
gastronomical delights.

6 Csalogány 26
MAP A3 ▪ I, Csalogány utca 26
▪ Open noon–3pm & 7–10pm Tue–
Sat ▪ www.csalogany26.hu ▪ FF

A modern restaurant serving simple
Mediterranean food, mostly grilled
on hot coals.

7 Hungarian Kitchen/21
MAP G2 ▪ I, Fortuna utca 21
▪ Open noon–midnight ▪ www.21
restaurant.hu ▪ FF

Here you'll enjoy a contemporary twist
on Hungarian cuisine. Dishes are
cooked using fresh market produce.

8 Alabárdos Étterem
MAP G2 ▪ I, Országház
utca 2 ▪ Open 7–11pm Mon–Fri,
noon–3pm & 7–11pm Sat ▪ www.
alabardos.hu ▪ FFF

Sensational Hungarian cuisine is
cooked in the traditional way by
an army of chefs *(see p55)*.

Chic interior of Arany Kaviár

9 Arany Kaviár
MAP G1 ▪ I, Ostrom utca 19
▪ 06 201 67 37 ▪ Open 6pm–midnight
Tue–Sun ▪ www.aranykaviar.hu ▪ FFF

The era of the Russian tsars is
conjured up with caviar, blinis
and champagne in truly opulent
surroundings *(see p54)*.

10 Café Pierrot
MAP G2 ▪ I, Fortuna utca 14
▪ 06 1 375 69 71 ▪ Open noon–midnight daily ▪ www.pierrot.hu ▪ FF

Founded as Budapest's first private
café-restaurant in 1982, this eatery
offers great food and service.

See map on p68

🔟 Gellért and Tabán

Ancient superstitions and medieval mysteries surround the areas of Gellért and Tabán. It is believed that Gellért Hill, which rises 140 m (460 ft) on the western bank of the Danube, was the scene of Bishop Gellért's death. In 1046, he was thrown from the top in a sealed barrel by enraged citizens for attempting to convert them to Christianity. The hill was later the site of the Habsburgs' monumental Citadel, built to quell revolt and assert control. At the foot of the hill, the luxurious Gellért Hotel and Baths Complex is a reminder of a gentler age. For centuries, Tabán was the city's most bohemian district, full of bars and gambling dens. More recently, urban planners have created parks and residential areas that now command some of the highest prices in the city.

Liberation Monument

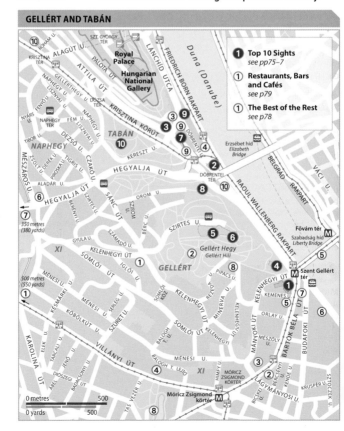

GELLÉRT AND TABÁN

1️⃣ **Top 10 Sights**
see pp75–7

1️⃣ **Restaurants, Bars and Cafés**
see p79

1️⃣ **The Best of the Rest**
see p78

0 metres 500
0 yards 500

Gellért Baths' main pool

1 Gellért Baths

Built in 1918, these are the best known and most luxurious baths *(see pp20–21)* in all of Budapest. There is a sublime main pool, with balconies, columns and stained-glass windows, as well as more traditional thermal baths. In summer, the open-air swimming pools at the back are popular with chess-playing pensioners – many spend all day here. Although the baths are attached to the Gellért Hotel, their entrance is on the side street.

2 Queen Elizabeth Monument
MAP J5

Although the wife of the Habsburg emperor, Franz József, was not Hungarian by birth, she adored her adopted subjects and made great efforts to soften Austrian attitudes towards Hungary. A number of streets, bridges and monuments throughout the nation are named after her. The monument dedicated to Elizabeth (Erzsébet) that overlooks the Danube from the Gellért embankment was designed by György Zala and erected in 1932. Its original home was on the other side of the river, but it was removed by the Communists in 1947. It wasn't until 1986 that the statue was reinstated at its present site.

3 Golden Stag House
MAP J4 ▪ I, Szarvas tér 1 ▪ 06 375 64 51 ▪ Open 11:30am–10pm daily ▪ www.aranyszarvasetterem.hu

This distinctive early 19th-century house, at the foot of Castle Hill, was named after the inn here – "Under the Golden Stag". A superb bas-relief above its entrance depicts a golden stag pursued by a pair of hunting hounds.

4 Cave Church
MAP K6 ▪ I, Szent Gellért rakpart 1 ▪ 0620 775 24 72 ▪ Open 9:30am–7:30pm Mon–Sat ▪ www. sziklatemplom.hu

On Easter Monday 1951, the Hungarian secret police arrested the Pauline monks at the Cave Church, murdering the leader Ferenc Vezér and sentencing the others to long prison sentences. The church was then bricked up and forgotten until August 1989. This remarkable place of worship, which is hewn into the Gellért hillside, was founded by monks of the Pauline Order after they visited Lourdes, France, in 1926. The revived order once again presides over the church, which is closed to the public when services are in progress.

Façade of the Cave Church

Weaponry at the Citadel

5 Citadel
MAP J–K6

Built to intimidate Budapest's citizens after the failed Uprising of 1848–9, the Citadel was never actually used for its original purpose – that of preventing new revolts – as the Hungarians sought their independence by more peaceful means. Although the country was granted partial independence according to the Dual Monarchy agreement of 1867, Austrian forces occupied the Citadel until 1897. The building is currently undergoing renovation to enhance the visitor experience, but its lookout points remain accessible and offer great views of the city.

6 Liberation Monument
MAP K6

One of the most visible landmarks in Budapest, this imposing cenotaph towers above the nearby Citadel. It was sculpted by Zsigmond Kisfaludi Stróbl and inaugurated in 1947, to commemorate the liberation of Budapest by Soviet forces. The inscription on the plinth once paid tribute to the Red Army, but was changed in 1992 and it now honours all those who "laid

Liberation Monument

BISHOP GELLÉRT

During a pagan revolt in the 11th century, Bishop Gellért was thrown off Old Hill in a sealed barrel. To seek forgiveness from God, the citizens of Budapest decided to dedicate the hill to him a century later. Of Italian descent, the Bishop had, in fact, been invited to Hungary to help the newly baptized St Stephen (István) spread Christianity throughout the region. It was rumoured that Stephen's brother, Prince Vata, had a hand in the martyrdom. Today, the Bishop is worshipped as Budapest's patron saint.

down their lives for Hungarian prosperity". Originally, a 6-m- (20-ft-) tall sculpture of a Soviet soldier equipped with a machine gun, with one of his fists clenched and the other holding a flag, stood at the foot of the monument, but this was later removed and relocated to Memento Park (see p102).

7 Tabán Parish Church
MAP J4 ■ I, Attila út 11
■ 06 1 375 54 91

This church is all that remains of Tabán's old district. Topped by a fine Neo-Baroque tower, it was built from 1728 to 1736 on the site of an earlier church that was converted into a mosque and later destroyed in the battle to overthrow the Ottoman Empire. Inside is a copy of the 12th-century carving, *Christ of Tabán*. The original is in the Castle Museum (see p69).

8 Gellért Monument
MAP J5

According to legend, the city's patron saint, Bishop Gellért was pushed off the hill that now bears his name for attempting

to convert Budapest's citizens to Christianity, including young Prince Imre, the son of Stephen I (István). Constructed in 1904, the monument to this Christian martyr is now looking a little the worse for wear, although it still retains its original majesty when viewed from afar. It is especially striking at night, when it is superbly lit. The statue and the enormous Neo-Classical colonnade that flanks it were designed by Gyula Jankovits and Imre Francsek.

View over Miklós Ybl Square

⑨ Miklós Ybl Square
MAP J4 ▪ I, Ybl Miklós tér

Arguably Hungary's greatest architect, known for gems such as St Stephen's Basilica (see pp16–17), Miklós Ybl is honoured with a commemorative statue which stands in a square bearing his name. It was designed by Ede Mayer and erected here in 1894, three years after Ybl died.

⑩ Tabán
MAP H4

There is little left of Tabán's original character, as its narrow streets on the slopes of Gellért Hill were cleared in 1910 to make way for terraces, gardens and Secession buildings. It was one of the first inhabited areas of Buda – the Celtic Eravi settled it from 1000 BC. The Romans later built a watchtower here and, in the 16th century, the Turks built the Rác Baths. In the 17th century, Tabán was home to Serb refugees, Greeks and Roma. Today, it is a popular venue for summer concerts, while in winter, the hillside is ideal for tobogganing.

A DAY IN GELLÉRT AND TABÁN

▶ MORNING

Start the day with a coffee and light breakfast on the corner terrace of the **Gellért Eszpresszó** (see p21) at the Gellért Hotel, then head around the corner to the **Gellért Hotel and Baths Complex** (see pp20–21). Try to resist the temptation to stay all day in the various baths and swimming pools; a few hours worth of pampering and a massage should be sufficient. Once refreshed, you'll be in fine form to tackle **Gellért Hill** (see p78) and climb up to the **Citadel**. After enjoying the views from its ramparts, break for lunch at Búsuló Juhász Étterem (see p79).

AFTERNOON

After lunch, descend southwards to the **Cave Church** (see p75), a bizarre place of worship hewn into the rock of Gellért Hill. From here, stroll down to Gellért Square and travel north along the embankment in the splendid tram No. 19 to **Miklós Ybl Square**. A short walk west leads you to the district of **Tabán**, where you'll be surrounded by Secession buildings. You can wander about the pretty terraces and gardens that replaced the earlier tenements. Next, visit the **Tabán Parish Church** just off Attila út, one of the few surviving buildings from Tabán's old district. To the north is the fascinating **Semmelweis Museum of Medical History** (see p78). End the day by enjoying a classic cake and a cup of coffee at Asztalka (see p79) in Dobrentei utca.

See map on p74 ←

The Best of the Rest

1 Sas Hill Nature Reserve

MAP N2 ▪ XI, Tájék utca 26
▪ 06 1 200 11 68 ▪ Opening times
vary, check website ▪ Adm
▪ www.dunaipoly.hu

A small reserve with a visitor centre
giving information on the rare plants,
insects and reptiles found here,
including the Pannonian lizard.

2 Gellért Hill

MAP J6

The views from Gellért Hill, especially
of the terraces below the Citadel, are
among the best in the city.

3 Semmelweis Museum of Medical History

MAP J4 ▪ I, Apród utca 1–3 ▪ 06 1 375
54 91 ▪ Open 10am–6pm Tue–Sun
▪ Adm ▪ www.semmelweismuseum.hu

The house of the ground-breaking
doctor Ignáz Semmelweis (1818–65)
is now a museum. Exhibits include
medicines from ancient Egypt to
the present day.

4 Cistercian Church of St Imre

MAP B6 ▪ XI, Villányi út 25
▪ 06 1 611 01 07

This Neo-Baroque church was built
in 1938. Inside are relics of St Imre,
patron saint of the Cistercian Order.

5 Liberty Bridge

MAP L6

Built between 1894 and 1899 by János
Feketeházy, this bridge (see p47) was
named after Emperor Franz József.

6 University of Technology and Economics

MAP C6 ▪ XI, Műegyetem rakpart 3
▪ 06 1 463 11 11 ▪ www.bme.hu

Hungary's largest academic
institution was built in 1904. Its
alumni include Ernő Rubik, the
inventor of the Rubik's Cube®.

7 Budapest Congress Center

MAP A5 ▪ XII, Jagelló út 1–3 ▪ 06 1
372 54 00 ▪ www.bcc.hu

Established in 1975, this arts complex
houses the Novotel Budapest Hotel
and conference rooms. It hosts
concerts and major exhibitions.

8 Former Swedish Embassy

MAP K6 ▪ XI, Minerva utca 3

This building was made famous by
Swedish diplomat Raoul Wallenberg,
who saved thousands of Jewish
prisoners from Nazi death camps.
A monument to him stands nearby.

9 Virág Benedek Building

MAP J4 ▪ Apród utca 10 ▪ 06 1
201 70 93 ▪ Open 2–6pm Wed, Fri & Sat,
11am–6pm Sun ▪ www.museum.hu

This is the only remnant of the old
Tabán area, which was detroyed by
fire in 1810. It hosts temporary
exhibitions usually themed around
the history of the area.

10 Rudas Baths

The luxurious Rudas Baths
(see p49), covered with a Turkish-
style dome, are among the oldest in
the city, dating from around 1550.

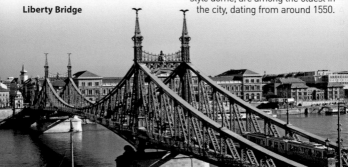

Liberty Bridge

Restaurants, Bars and Cafés

1 Búsuló Juhász Étterem
MAP B6 ▪ XI, Kelenhegyi út 58
▪ 06 209 16 49 ▪ Open noon–11pm
daily ▪ www.busulojuhasz.hu ▪ FFF

The slopes of Gellért Hill provide a
fabulous location for this traditional
Hungarian restaurant *(see p55)*, which
specializes in game dishes.

2 Marcello
MAP C6 ▪ XI, Bartók Béla út 40
▪ Open 11:30am–10pm Mon–Wed,
11:30am–11pm Thu–Sat, noon–10pm
Sun ▪ www.marcelloetterem.hu ▪ FF

A somewhat spartan pizzeria serving
delicious thin and crispy pizzas at
remarkably low prices.

3 La Nube
MAP C6 ▪ XI, Bartók Béla út
41 ▪ Open 4:30–11pm Mon–Fri,
12:30–11pm Sat & Sun ▪ www.
lanubecafe.com ▪ FF

Tapas and wine bar serving huge
platters of fine cheese, cold meats
and seafood. There are plenty of
options for vegans too.

**4 Zileat Brunch &
Bistro**
MAP J4 ▪ I, Döbrentei utca
22 ▪ Open 8:30am–9pm
daily ▪ www.zileat.hu ▪ F

A fabulous range of brunch
dishes is served here
alongside homemade cakes
in a bright and colourful setting.

Cakes in Asztalka

5 Szeged Étterem
MAP C6 ▪ XI, Bartók Béla út 1
▪ 06 1 209 16 68 ▪ Open noon–11pm
daily ▪ FF

A Hungarian restaurant next to the
Gellért Hotel. The food is very good,
and river-fish dishes are the speciality.

6 János Étterem
MAP A5 ▪ XI, Hegyalja út 23
▪ 06 1 202 34 14 ▪ Open noon–
11:30pm daily ▪ FFF

A surprisingly good eatery in a rather
nondescript hotel. The menu is mainly
made up of Hungarian classics.

The elegant dining room of Palack Bobar

7 Palack Borbar
MAP K6 ▪ XI, Szent Gellért tér 3
▪ Open noon–midnight Tue–Sat,
noon–10pm Sun & Mon ▪ www.
palackborbar.hu ▪ FF

There are some great wines on offer
here. It also serves tasty homemade
cakes and specially blended coffee.

8 Hemingway Étterem
MAP P2 ▪ XI, Kosztolányi Dezső
tér 2 ▪ 06 1 381 05 22 ▪ Open noon–
midnight Mon–Sat, noon–4pm Sun
▪ www.hemingway-etterem.hu ▪ FF

Escape the bustle of downtown with
a mojito or a cigar on the terrace at
this great seafood restaurant.

9 Asztalka
MAP J4 ▪ I, Döbrentei
utca 15 ▪ 06 20 581 33 99
▪ Open 11am–6pm Wed–Fri,
11am–7pm Sat & Sun ▪ F

This busy little café offers
a choice of gourmet coffees.
The selection of cakes at
this place changes daily.

10 Déryné Bisztró
MAP G3 ▪ I, Krisztina tér 3 ▪ 06
1 225 14 07 ▪ Opening times vary,
check website ▪ www.deryne.com ▪ FF

Popular with the locals, this family-
friendly, French-style bistro is often
packed for brunch at the weekend.

See map on p74

🔟 Around Parliament

The Buda Castle may have the benefit of its location on top of Castle Hill, but the city's defining sight remains its splendid Parliament building. The area around Parliament is redolent with history and power, with large squares, wide avenues and Secession architecture – remnants of the once powerful Austro-Hungarian Empire. Several of the city's most important buildings, including St Stephen's Basilica and the outstanding Hungarian State Opera, are located here. The area is also home to some of Budapest's finest restaurants, as well as its most exclusive shops and residences.

KOSSUTH

Monument to Lajos Kossuth in Kossuth Lajos Square

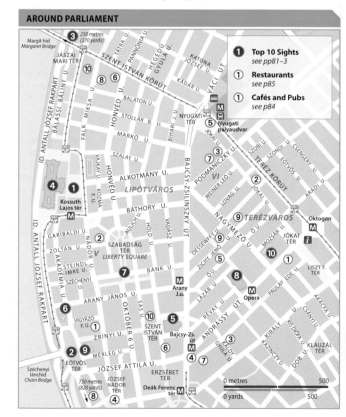

AROUND PARLIAMENT

1	**Top 10 Sights** see pp81–3
①	**Restaurants** see p85
①	**Cafés and Pubs** see p84

1 Kossuth Lajos Square

MAP K1 ■ V, Kossuth Lajos tér

Still considered the best address in the city, Budapest's finest square is surrounded on all sides by splendid buildings. It was developed at the end of the 19th century, following the unification of Buda and Pest. The square is named after Lajos Kossuth, who led the 1848–9 Uprising against the Habsburgs and subsequently became a member of Hungary's first democratic government. He was exiled in 1849 after the Uprising was suppressed. A monument in front of the Parliament commemorates the Uprising. Opposite is another that pays tribute to Ferenc II Rákóczi, leader of the 1703 revolt against Austrian rule. A memorial to Imre Nagy, prime minister and leader of the 1956 revolt against the Soviet Union, also stands nearby.

2 Széchenyi István Square

MAP K3 ■ V, Széchenyi István tér

This square has had various names: first called Unloading Square, it was renamed Franz József Square to mark the coronation. From 1947 to 2011 it was named after US president Franklin D Roosevelt and it is today named after the founder of the Academy of Sciences. The square features several fine hotels, including the Gresham Palace (see p83).

3 Margaret Island

MAP B1

Inhabited as far back as Roman times, Margaret Island (see pp22–3), a tranquil oasis in the middle of the Danube, is a beautiful green space that has been open to the public since 1869. The 3-km (2-mile) long island served as a popular hunting ground for medieval kings, while monks were drawn to its peaceful setting. Today the island still offers the perfect escape after sightseeing in the busy city.

Lush foliage at Margaret Island

4 Hungarian Parliament

Constructed in 1902 to house the National Assembly, Hungary's Parliament building (see pp12–15) remains the city's primary source of civic pride. It was designed by Imre Steindl, a professor at Budapest's University of Technology and Economics, who won an open competition held to find an architect for the building. Inspired by London's Houses of Parliament, this magnificent edifice is filled with paintings, frescoes and tapestries by renowned Hungarian artists. The interior can only be seen on one of the guided tours, which take place when Parliament is not in session.

Hungarian Parliament building

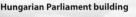

The impressive and colourful nave of St Stephen's Basilica

5 St Stephen's Basilica

Visible from all over the city, the dome of St Stephen's Basilica is exactly the same height as the Parliament's own dome. Construction of the basilica began in 1851 but its completion was delayed after the original dome collapsed in 1868; it was finally completed in 1905. Today, it is one of the city's most sacred sites, as it houses the mummified right hand of St Stephen (István).

6 Academy of Sciences

MAP K2 ■ V, Széchenyi István tér 9 ■ 06 1 411 64 89 ■ Open 9am–4pm Mon–Fri ■ www.mta.hu

Inaugurated in 1864, the Academy of Sciences is a classic piece of Neo-Renaissance architecture designed by Friedrich Stüler. The statues on the façade, including those of Isaac Newton and René Descartes, are by Miklós Izsó and Emil Wolff, while the interior features more statues by Izsó.

7 Liberty Square

MAP K2 ■ V, Szabadság tér

Laid out in 1886 on the site of the barracks that housed the Austrian army, Liberty Square has long been synonymous with Hungary's freedom struggle. The first prime minister of independent Hungary, Count Lajos Batthyány, was executed in the barracks on 6 Oct 1849. The square was also the site of the 1956 protests against the Soviet Union. Today, an eternal flame at the corner of Aulich utca and Hold utca pays tribute to Batthyány, while the statue on the northern side honours Soviet troops who liberated the city in 1944–5.

8 Hungarian State Opera

This stunning building (see pp32–3) is one of Europe's finest concert halls, and the best way to see it is by attending a performance. World-class operas and ballets are performed almost every evening, and tickets are very reasonably priced.

Hungarian State Opera auditorium

SIR THOMAS GRESHAM

Although one of the city's finest buildings bears his name, Sir Thomas Gresham (**below**) never set foot in Budapest. Gresham Palace was commissioned over 300 years after his death by the insurance company he had established. The principal figure in the founding of the London Royal Exchange, Gresham is best remembered for the maxim he made famous: "bad money drives out good".

A DAY AROUND PARLIAMENT

MORNING

Start with a sandwich or one of the excellent sweets at the **Szamos Today** café *(Kossuth Lajos tér 10; 06 269 02 16; open 7:30am–7pm daily)* next to the Kossuth Lajos tér metro station. Follow this with a leisurely stroll, crossing **Kossuth Lajos Square** *(see p81)* to the sensational **Hungarian Parliament** *(see pp12–15)*. Here you can join one of several guided tours, which are the only way to see the building. After this, walk along the scenic Danube embankment to **Széchenyi István Square** at the head of the **Chain Bridge** *(see p47)*. You can end with a light lunch on the terrace of the **Four Seasons Hotel Gresham Palace**.

AFTERNOON

Walk along **Zrinyi utca**, one of Budapest's foremost residential streets, famous for its smart Secessionist-style apartment buildings, to the magnificent **St Stephen's Basilica** *(see pp16–17)* on St Stephen's Square. Climb the steps to the top of the church's dome for splendid views of the city. Then head to the **Hungarian State Opera** *(see pp32–3)*, timing your arrival to coincide with one of the daily guided tours at 3pm and 4pm. Eat an early dinner at the popular **Klassz** *(see p85)* and then prepare for a night at the Opera (make sure you reserve tickets in advance). Afterwards, a drink at nearby **Boutiq'Bar** *(see p84)* will round off a splendid day.

9 Gresham Palace
MAP K3 ■ V, Széchenyi István tér 5–7 ■ 06 1 268 60 00 ■ Open 24 hours daily ■ www.fourseasons.com/budapest

Designed by Zsigmond Quittner and the brothers József and László Vágó in 1907, Gresham Palace enjoys one of Budapest's best locations opposite the Chain Bridge. It is an imposing edifice with several Secessionist features, from stained-glass windows (including one featuring a portrait of the patriot Lajos Kossuth), to its high atrium and chandelier. Today it houses a Four Seasons hotel *(see p116)*.

10 Operetta Theatre
MAP M2 ■ VI, Nagymező utca 17 ■ 06 1 472 20 30 ■ By appointment only ■ www.operett.hu

Operettas (one-act or light operas) have been performed here since 1898, when the building opened as the Orfeum Theatre. Designed by Viennese architects Fellner and Helmer, it was modified and renamed the Operetta Theatre in 1923, as it provided a home for the thriving operetta scene. It was further renovated in 1999–2001, but the interior remained faithful to the original design.

See map on p80 ←

Cafés and Pubs

1 Ötkert
MAP K2 ■ V, Zrínyi utca 4 ■ 06 1 330 86 52 ■ Open noon–midnight Sun–Tue, noon–4am Wed & Thu, noon–5am Fri & Sat

This hip designer bar (see p56) is modelled on the ruined-garden bars typical of the seventh district.

Courtyard at trendy Ötkert

2 La Delizia
MAP M1 ■ Jókai utca 13 ■ 06 30 641 52 06 ■ Open 10am–8pm Mon–Sat

This small shop and café sells handmade cookies and healthy, sugar-, lactose- and gluten-free desserts.

3 Desszert.Neked
MAP M2 ■ Paulay Ede utca 17 ■ 0620 253 15 19 ■ Open 11am–9pm Mon–Fri, 10am–9pm Sat, Sun

This café offers new-wave French and Hungarian pastries. Many best-known local cakes get a modern twist.

4 Vakegér Tőzsdekocsma
MAP M2 ■ VI, Paulay Ede utca 2 ■ 06 70 333 96 33 ■ Open 6pm–2am Sun–Thu, 6pm–5am Fri–Sat

At the "Blind Mouse Stock Exchange Pub", prices rise and fall depending on how often a particular drink is bought.

5 The Box Donut
MAP L1 ■ Teréz körút 62 ■ Open 7:42am–8:08pm Mon–Sat, 9:42am–8:08pm Sun

They serve square-shaped handmade doughnuts in 25 flavours, plus sandwiches and coffee.

6 Európa Kávéház
MAP C2 ■ Szent István Krt 7–9 ■ 06 1 312 23 62 ■ Open 7am–8pm daily

Classic café serving pastries, cakes and at least eight different kinds of hot chocolate.

7 Boutiq'Bar
MAP L3 ■ VI, Paulay Ede utca 5 ■ 0630 229 18 21 ■ Open 6pm–late Tue–Sat

Boutiq'Bar (see p57) gets very busy after 9pm, thanks to its excellent cocktails made by expert bartenders.

8 Tóth Kocsma
MAP C2 ■ V, Falk Miksa utca 17 ■ 06 1 302 64 42 ■ Open 3pm–midnight Mon–Fri (from 5pm Sat)

This is very much a quintessential Budapest pub (see p56). A must if you want a pint or a *palinka* with the locals. Try the elderflower cider.

9 AlterEgo
MAP C3 ■ VI, Dessewffy utca 33 ■ Open 10pm–5am Fri & Sat ■ www.alteregoclub.hu

Budapest's leading LGBTQ+ bar and club (see p56) plays classic pop hits and welcomes everyone. The drag shows here are enormously popular.

10 Tokaji Borozó
MAP C3 ■ V, Falk Miksa utca 32 ■ 06 1 269 31 43 ■ Open 1–11pm Mon–Fri

This Hungarian wine bar is dedicated to the famed sweet dessert wines that are sold under the Tokaji name.

Restaurants

PRICE CATEGORIES
For a three-course meal for one, with half a bottle of wine (or equivalent meal), taxes and extra charges.

F under Ft5,000   **FF** Ft5,000–10,000
FFF over Ft10,000

1 Klassz
**MAP M2 ■ VI, Andrássy út 41
■ Open 11:30am–11pm daily ■ FF**
A modern bistro offering international dishes, made using local ingredients, and excellent wines. No reservations.

2 Iguana
**MAP K2 ■ V, Zoltán utca 16
■ 06 1 331 43 52 ■ Open 11:30–12:30am daily ■ FF**
Great Tex-Mex fare in a lively setting. Fajitas, tortillas and burritos come in large portions at reasonable prices.

3 Ape Regina Restaurant & Bar
**MAP L1 ■ Podmaniczky utca 18
■ 0630 779 75 45 ■ Open noon–midnight daily ■ FF**
Ape Regina is an all-you-can-eat Italian restaurant. Some drinks are also included in the fixed price.

4 Onyx Restaurant
**MAP K3 ■ V, Vörösmarty tér 7–8
■ Open noon–2:30pm & 6:30–11pm Tue–Fri, 6:30–11pm Sat
■ www.onyxrestaurant.hu ■ FFF**
Enjoy the haute cuisine without spending a fortune by selecting one of the set menus (see p54).

5 Imázs Restaurant
MAP L2 ■ 1065, Hajós utca 16–18 ■ 06 1 269 32 63 ■ Open daily ■ FF
Located in the heart of Budapest, this restaurant serves great Thai and Japanese cuisine.

6 Stradivari Restaurant
**MAP L3 ■ Hercegprímás utca 5
■ 0630 438 88 24 ■ FFF**
This stylish restaurant in the Aria hotel offers bistro-style dining.

Afterwards, enjoy drinks at the High Note SkyBar on the top floor while taking in the splendid city panorama.

7 Sir Lancelot
MAP C3 ■ VI, Podmaniczky utca 14 ■ 06 1 302 44 56 ■ Open noon–1am ■ FF
This themed restaurant serves huge portions of medieval dishes, from marrow bones and pork knuckles to whole geese and chickens.

8 Kollázs
**MAP K3 ■ V, Széchenyi István tér 5–6 ■ 06 268 51 84
■ Open 6:30–1am daily ■ FF**
At Kollázs (see p55), you can dine on clever, inventive dishes or enjoy the simpler delights.

Elegant interior of Kollázs

9 Drop Glutenfree Restaurant
MAP L3 ■ VI, Hajós u. 27 ■ 06 1 235 04 68 ■ Open 7:30am–midnight ■ FF
An extensive gluten- and lactose-free menu coupled with a terrific selection of drinks makes this restaurant a local favourite.

10 Café Kör
MAP L3 ■ V, Sas utca 17 ■ 06 1 311 00 53 ■ Open 10am–10pm Mon–Sat ■ FF
This eatery is legendary among the expat community, who flock here for light meals, good drinks and great atmosphere. Note that credit cards are not accepted.

See map on p80

🔟 Central Pest

Most visitors to Budapest head straight for this area, known as Belváros or the Inner City. It is the city's commercial hub, and is filled with fine buildings, shops and cafés. The area lay in ruins at the end of the 17th century, and was only redeveloped in the 19th century when many of Pest's most important buildings were built, including the Hungarian National Museum. Today, many of the streets and squares are entirely pedestrianized, making it an ideal place for walking, shopping and dining outdoors. In fact, during the summer, the southern end of Váci Street becomes a never-ending melee of cafés and pubs, with revellers drinking on the pavements from dawn to dusk.

Artifact in the Hungarian National Museum

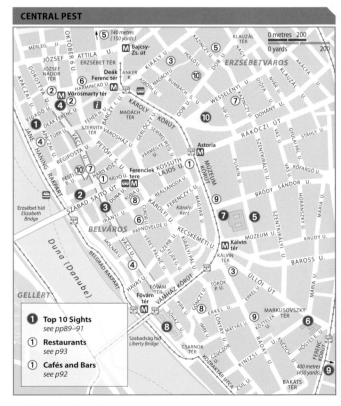

CENTRAL PEST

❶ Top 10 Sights
see pp89–91

① Restaurants
see p93

① Cafés and Bars
see p92

Erzsébet híd Elizabeth Bridge

Szabadság híd Liberty Bridge

Previous pages The Fishermen's Bastion

1 Vigadó Square
MAP K4 ■ V, Vigadó tér

Facing the Danube, Vigadó Square is one of Budapest's quietest spots. It is dominated by the Vigadó Concert Hall, under whose sublime colonnades visitors seek shade during hot summer afternoons. Built between 1859 and 1864 and designed by Frigyes Feszl, it replaced an earlier hall that was destroyed during the 1848–9 Uprising. The façade is a wonder of arched windows, statues and busts. In the centre is a Hungarian coat of arms. Badly damaged in World War II, restoration efforts have faithfully returned the building to its former glory. Facing the Hall is the Modernist Budapest Marriott Hotel (see p116), built in 1969. The jetties on the square's embankment are the departure point for Danube river cruises.

2 Inner City Parish Church
MAP K4 ■ V, Március 15 tér 2 ■ 06 1 318 31 08 ■ Open 9am–7pm daily

Pest's oldest church has a long and varied history. The original Roman-style structure was decimated by the Tartars, and its 14th-century replacement was converted into a mosque by the Turks. It was nearly destroyed again after World War II,

when builders wanted to demolish it to make way for the Elizabeth Bridge. Luckily, it was saved at the last minute, but the proximity of the approach road to its walls shows what a close call it was.

Pedestrianized Váci Street

3 Váci Street
One of Pest's oldest streets, Váci Street (see pp18–19) originally led to the town of Vác (see p65). As Pest prospered, so did the street, and it soon became a favourite among Budapest's wealthy citizens. The goods stores gave way to exclusive boutiques, and today it is one of the city's most popular shopping venues. The northern half is dominated by retail outlets and department stores. The pedestrianized southern end of Váci Street is home to some of the area's best cafés and clubs. The street has become increasingly touristy in recent decades, but has nevertheless retained its eclectic feel.

4 Vörösmarty Square
MAP K3 ■ V, Vörösmarty tér

This splendid pedestrian plaza is named after the poet Mihály Vörösmarty, whose statue stands at its centre. Designed by Ede Telcs and built in Carrara marble, the statue rallies the nation in the poet's own words: "Your homeland, Hungary, serve unwaveringly". The square's northern side is dominated by Gerbeaud Cukrászda (see pp18 & 57), Hungary's most famous coffee house. It is also worth visiting the quaint metro station.

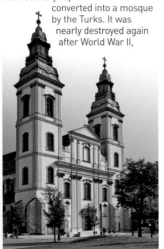
Façade of the Inner City Parish Church

JEWISH QUARTER

Budapest's Jewish Quarter is based immediately north of Károly körút. The community thrived here until 1941, when anti-Semitic laws were passed by the government of Admiral Horthy. By 1944 much of the area was a ghetto, and thousands were deported to death camps. Today the community is once again growing and thriving, with synagogues, shops and kosher restaurants.

5 Mihály Pollack Square
MAP D5 ■ V, Pollack Mihály tér

Named after the architect of several Neo-Classical buildings including the National Museum, this square is famous for its three palaces – Count Károlyi at No. 6, Prince Eszterházy at No. 8 and Prince Festetics at No. 10. The superb façades of the palaces (of which only the Festetics Palace is open to the public), make the square one of the most picturesque in the city.

6 Museum of Applied Arts
MAP D5 ■ IX, Üllői út 33–7 ■ 06 1 456 51 07 ■ Closed for renovation ■ www.imm.hu

The opening of this museum was the finale of the city's 1896 Millennium celebrations. Created to house the Hungarian State's sizeable collection of art, the exquisite building was designed by Ödön Lechner and Gyula Pártos. Like many Secessionist buildings, it incorporates elements

Dome of the Museum of Applied Arts

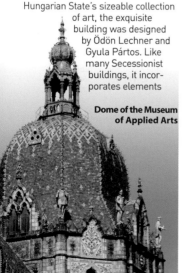

inspired from Asian art and architecture, such as the green domes and the glass-roofed courtyard. The museum features fine arts, crafts and traditional costumes.

Hungarian National Museum

7 Hungarian National Museum

The National Museum (see pp34–5) was founded in 1802, and owes its existence to Count Ferenc Széchényi (see p35), who donated his collections of books and art to the nation. The building was designed by Mihály Pollack and completed in 1845. In 1848, it was the scene of a historic event, when Sándor Petőfi recited his poem Nemzeti Dal (National Song) from the steps, thus igniting the Uprising of 1848–9. The event is re-enacted each year. The museum is the richest source of art and artifacts anywhere in the country.

8 Corvinus University of Budapest
MAP L6 ■ V, Fővám tér 8 ■ 06 1 482 50 00

A Neo-Renaissance masterpiece, this university was built between 1871 and 1874 to house the city's main customs house. Designed by Miklós Ybl, its Danube façade is set on three levels – a colonnade supporting a balcony, with two rows of arched windows facing the river. The balustrade supports 10 allegorical figures sculpted by August Sommer. The building became the University of Economics in 1951, when it was named after Karl Marx; a statue of Marx still stands in the building. In 2000, it was given its current name.

9 Holocaust Memorial Center

MAP E6 ■ IX, Páva utca 39 ■ 06 1 455
33 33 ■ Open 10am–6pm Tue–Sun
■ Adm ■ www.hdke.hu

This centre was founded both in order
to collect and study material relating
to the history of the Holocaust, and
to honour its victims. The persecution
and suffering of Hungarian Jews
and the Roma community during
the Holocaust is examined through
a permanent exhibition, with special
attention paid to the relationship
between the state and its citizens.
The centre also contains an
8-m- (26-ft-) high glass Wall of
Remembrance on which it is hoped
that the name of every Hungarian
victim of the Holocaust will one day
be engraved. There's also a restored
synagogue, dating from 1924, which
now hosts temporary exhibitions.

The *Tree of Life*, a Holocaust memorial
outside the Great Synagogue

10 Great Synagogue

Built in Byzantine style by
Viennese architect Ludwig Förster
in 1854–9, the largest synagogue in
Europe can hold over 3,000 people
(see pp36–7). It houses the Hungarian
Jewish Museum (see p44), which
chronicles the long history of the city's
Jews. At the rear of the Synagogue is
the Raoul Wallenberg Memorial Park,
which features the *Tree of Life*, a
Holocaust memorial. Designed by
Imre Varga, each leaf of this silver
weeping willow tree bears the name
of one of the 600,000 Hungarian
Jews killed during the Holocaust.

A DAY IN DOWNTOWN BUDAPEST

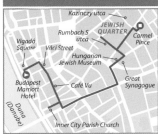

MORNING

A leisurely cup of coffee on
the terrace of the Modernist
Budapest Marriott Hotel (see
p116) on Vigadó Square will set
the tone for the day. Then walk
a short distance east to **Váci
Street** (see pp18–19), with its
superb retail stores on the
northern side, including souvenir
stalls, clothes chains and high-
end fashion brands. Next, visit
Pest's oldest church, the **Inner
City Parish Church** (see p89)
just off Szabad Sajtó út, before
stopping to enjoy a light lunch
at **Café Vu** (Mercure Budapest
City Center).

AFTERNOON

After lunch, either take the metro
from Ferenciek tere up to Astoria
or walk ten minutes along the
busy Kossuth Lajos utca to the
Great Synagogue on Dohány
utca. You can visit the splendid
Byzantine-inspired synagogue
and its excellent **Hungarian
Jewish Museum** (see p44) before
paying your respects to the Jews
killed in the Holocaust at the
sobering *Tree of Life* memorial in
the **Raoul Wallenberg Memorial
Park**, located in the courtyard at
the back of the synagogue. Then
set about exploring the rest of
the fascinating **Jewish Quarter**,
which is known for its little gift
shops and quaint book stores, as
well as the far less ostentatious
synagogues on Rumbach S utca
and Kazinczy utca. End your day
with a delicious glatt-kosher
dinner at the **Carmel Pince**
restaurant (Kazinczy utca 31).

See map on p88

Cafés and Bars

① Café Astoria
MAP M4 ▪ V, Kossuth Lajos utca 19–21 ▪ 06 1 889 60 22 ▪ Open 7am–11pm daily

An elegant café in the Hotel Astoria that manages to turn a cup of coffee into an event.

Opulent interior of Café Astoria

② Gerbeaud Cukrászda
MAP K3 ▪ V, Vörösmarty tér 7 ▪ 06 429 90 00 ▪ Open 9am–9pm daily

Beautifully decorated cakes complement the interior of the city's most famous café (see p57).

③ Spíler BistroPub
MAP M3 ▪ Király utca 13, Gozsdu udvar ▪ 06 1 878 13 09 ▪ Open 11:30am–midnight Sun–Thu (to 1am Fri & Sat)

Comprises two venues in the Gozsdu Courtyard – Spíler Classic is a gastropub with retro elements of Communist Hungary, while Spíler Shanghai is more like a speakeasy.

④ 1000 Tea
MAP L5 ▪ V, Váci utca 65 ▪ 06 1 337 82 17 ▪ Open noon–9pm Mon–Sat ▪ www.1000tea.hu

This café serves a range of teas. With soothing music, it is the perfect place to while away an afternoon.

⑤ Kőleves (Stonesoup)
MAP M3 ▪ VII, Kazinczy utca 37–41 ▪ Opening times vary, check website ▪ www.kolevesvendeglo.hu

Good bar and restaurant with a fabulous terrace popular with families.

⑥ Good Spirit Bar
MAP C5 ▪ V, Veres Pálné u. 7 ▪ Open 5pm–1am Wed–Sat ▪ www.goodspiritbar.hu

Possibly Budapest's only bar with a huge array of whiskies and bottled beers. They serve a variety of cocktails with snacks.

⑦ Szimpla Kert
MAP M3 ▪ VII, Kazinczy utca 14 ▪ Open 3pm–4am Mon–Thu, noon–4am Fri–Sun ▪ www.szimpla.hu

Housed in a refurbished apartment block, Szimpla Kert (see p56) is the biggest ruined-garden bar in the seventh district.

⑧ Chloe Café
MAP L4 ▪ V, Irányi utca 18 ▪ Open 10am–7:30pm Wed–Sat (to 5pm Sun) ▪ www.chloecafe.hu

A stylish café and wine bar with a variety of champagne served by the glass, plus croissants and salads topped with forest fruit dressings.

⑨ Paris, Texas
MAP D5 ▪ IX, Ráday utca 22 ▪ 06 1 218 05 70 ▪ Open 5pm–2am daily

A late-night hotspot for those who like to stop for a nightcap on their way home. The Texan link is reinforced by the range of malt whiskies on offer.

⑩ Doblo
MAP M3 ▪ VII, Dob utca 20 ▪ 0620 398 88 63 ▪ Open 2pm–1am daily

Wines from all over the world can be sampled at this elegant bar (see p56).

Customers enjoy fine wines at Doblo

Restaurants

1 Apostolok
MAP L4 ▪ V, Kígyó utca 4–6
▪ Open 11:30am–11:30pm daily
▪ www.apostoloketterem.hu ▪ FFF

This restaurant in the heart of the
city opened as a pub in 1902. It offers
traditional Hungarian flavours.

2 Vapiano
MAP C4 ▪ V, Vörösmarty tér 3
▪ Open 11am–11pm Mon–Sat (to
9pm Sun) ▪ www.vapiano.hu ▪ FFF

Enjoy fabulous views of Vörösmarty
Square while tucking into delicious
Italian food.

3 Costes
MAP M5 ▪ IX, Ráday utca 4
▪ Open 6:30pm–midnight Wed–Sun
▪ www.costes.hu ▪ FFF

White-gloved waiters glide from
table to table at this chic, Michelin-
starred restaurant *(see p54)* that's
at the forefront of Budapest's contemporary fine-dining scene.

4 DNB Restaurant
MAP C4 ▪ V, Duna korzó
(Marriott Hotel) ▪ Open 6:30am–11pm
daily ▪ www.dnbbudapest.com ▪ FFF

Adopting a farm-to-table concept,
this restaurant serves delicious,
seasonal dishes made with locally
sourced ingredients, such as the
wild boar striploin steak. The Sunday
brunch here is a favourite.

5 Comme Chez Soi
MAP K4 ▪ V, Aranykéz utca 2
▪ Open noon–11pm Tue–Sat ▪ www.
commechezsoi.hu ▪ FFF

Fine Italian cuisine makes up the
menu at this charming little place. You
will need to reserve a table a day or
two in advance, but its worth the wait.

6 Nobu
MAP K3 ▪ V, Kempinski Hotel
Corvinus, Erzsébet tér 7–8 ▪ Open
noon–3pm & 6–11:45pm daily
▪ www.noburestaurants.com ▪ FFF

Known for its delectable sushi bar, luxurious Nobu attracts an elite crowd.

7 Kiosk Budapest
MAP L4 ▪ V, Március 15 tér 4
▪ Open noon–midnight daily
▪ www.kiosk-budapest.hu ▪ FFF

Once a warehouse, this vast space
has been converted into a trendy bar
and restaurant serving simple but
beautifully presented food, including
one of the best burgers in the city.

Galleried interior at Borbíróság

8 Borbíróság
MAP M6 ▪ IX, Csarnoktér 5 ▪ 06
1 219 09 02 ▪ Open 8am–11:30pm
Mon–Sat ▪ www.borbirosag.hu ▪ FF

The "law courts of wine" venue has a
legal theme and a vast array of mainly
Hungarian wines on offer.

9 Múzeum Kávéház és Étterem
MAP M4 ▪ VIII, Múzeum körút 12 ▪ 06
1 338 42 21 ▪ Open 6pm–midnight
Mon–Sat ▪ FFF

This 1855 former coffee house is next
to the National Museum and serves
delicious Hungarian specialities.

10 Babel
MAP L4 ▪ V, Piarista köz 2
▪ Open 6pm–midnight Tue–Sat
▪ www.babel-budapest.hu ▪ FFF

At the foot of the Elizabeth Bridge,
this bistro/delicatessen offers fresh
ingredients and attentive service.

See map on p88

TOP10 Around City Park

Home to some of the finest buildings and widest boulevards in the city, the area around City Park (Városliget) is where the citizens of Budapest have long come to play. Everything is built on a gloriously grand scale, from the cafés and bistros of Liszt Ferenc tér to the mansions of Andrássy Avenue and Városligeti Terrace, and even the City Park itself – fronted by the magnificent Millennium Monument. City Park was chosen as the centre of the city's 1896 Millennium Celebrations *(see p96)*, and among the many splendid buildings constructed especially for the event were the Museum of Fine Arts and Vajdahunyad Castle.

Detail of the Millennium Monument

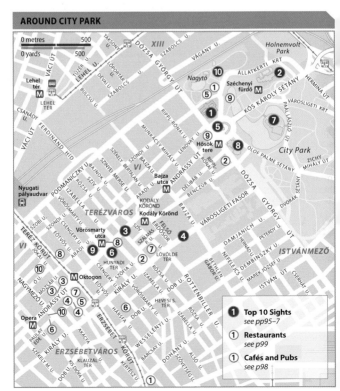

AROUND CITY PARK

1 Top 10 Sights
see pp95–7

① Restaurants
see p99

① Cafés and Pubs
see p98

1 Museum of Fine Arts

MAP E2 ▪ XIV, Hősök tere, Dózsa György út 41 ▪ Open 10am–6pm Tue–Sun ▪ www.szepmuveszeti.hu ▪ Adm

Hungary's largest collection of international art is housed in a 1906 building designed by Fülöp Herzog and Albert Schikendanz. It has works by Raphael, Goya and Velázquez, and a collection of El Grecos. The museum shares its collection with the Hungarian National Gallery (see pp26–9).

Outdoor pools, Széchenyi Baths

2 Széchenyi Baths

MAP F2 ▪ XIV, Állatkerti út 11 ▪ 06 1 363 32 10 ▪ Open thermal pool: 6am–7pm daily; swimming pool and steam rooms: 6am–10pm daily ▪ Adm ▪ www.szechenyibath.com

Opened in 1913, Széchenyi (see p48) is a vast complex of indoor and outdoor pools, which include Hungary's deepest and hottest thermal baths. Immensely popular all year round, this is where people come to find the classic Hungarian bathing experience.

3 Andrássy Avenue

MAP L2, M2

A long, wide boulevard from City Park to the city centre, Andrássy Avenue, or Andrássy út, is Budapest's most exclusive address. It is lined with restaurants, theatres and shops, as well as the State Opera (see pp32–3). At No. 22 is the Drechsler Palace, built by the Hungarian Railways as rental apartments for its pension fund in 1883, before being used later

as the Hungarian Ballet Academy. The building is currently empty, but there are plans to turn it into a luxury hotel. The House of Terror Museum (see p97) is further down the street, at No. 60. Under Andrássy Avenue runs the Metro 1, Hungary's oldest and the world's second-oldest underground railway. It was declared a UNESCO World Heritage Site in 2002.

4 Városligeti Terrace

MAP E3

This serene tree-lined avenue is the gentle counterpart to the more commercial Andrássy Avenue. Numerous embassies line the avenue, and there are two significant churches in the street: a Calvinist one at the southern end and a Lutheran one towards City Park.

5 Heroes' Square

MAP E2 ▪ Hősök tere

Heroes' Square was laid out during the 1890s and was the focal point of Hungary's Millennium Celebrations in 1896 (held to mark 1,000 years since the Magyar conquest of the Carpathian Basin). At its heart is the 36-m (110-ft) Millennium Monument, flanked by two colonnades. The riders on horseback at the foot of the monument represent the seven chieftains of the seven Magyar tribes that settled in Hungary.

Millennium Monument at Heroes' Square

Pianos in the Franz Liszt Museum

6 Franz Liszt Museum

MAP D3 ▪ VI, Vörösmarty utca 35 ▪ 06 1 322 98 04 ▪ Open 10am–6pm Mon–Fri, 9am–5pm Sat ▪ Adm ▪ www.lisztmuseum.hu

More famously known to the world by his Germanic name of Franz, Ferenc Liszt was Hungary's greatest composer. He lived here from 1881 until his death in 1886. The house became a museum in 1986 and the furniture, pianos and manuscripts give an insight into the life and work of this musically talented man.

7 Vajdahunyad Castle

MAP F2 ▪ Museum of Agriculture: 06 1 422 07 65; open 10am–5pm Tue–Sun; adm

In the middle of City Park is the incredible Vajdahunyad Castle, a mixture of Renaissance, Gothic, Baroque and Romanesque styles, designed by Ignác Alpár for the Millennium Celebrations. Alpár's idea was to

illustrate the entire evolution of Hungarian architecture in a single construction. To achieve this, each section reflects an important edifice and, all in all, the castle represents over 20 famous Hungarian buildings. The Museum of Agriculture in the Baroque section is the only part of the castle that is open to the public.

8 Műcsarnok (Kunsthalle)

MAP E2 ▪ XIV, Hősök tere ▪ 06 1 460 70 00 ▪ Open 10am–6pm Tue–Sun, noon–8pm Thu ▪ Adm ▪ www.mucsarnok.hu

Facing the Museum of Fine Arts, the Műcsarnok (literally "art hall") was completed in 1895. The imposing building, dominated by its portico with six supporting columns, was designed by Fülöp Herzog and Albert Schikendanz. Today, it hosts temporary exhibitions and concerts.

Vajdahunyad Castle

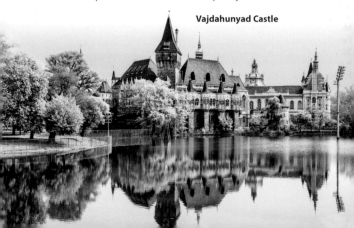

9 House of Terror Museum

MAP D3 ▪ VI, Andrássy út 60 ▪ 06 1 374 26 00 ▪ Open 10am–6pm Tue–Sun ▪ Adm ▪ www.terrorhaza.hu

This building *(see p45)* was the head-quarters of the fascist Arrow Cross before and during World War II, and the secret police afterwards. Exhibits include a T54 tank used in the repression of the 1956 revolution. In the basement, used as a prison during both regimes, one cell has been recreated to look just as it did in the 1940s.

House of Terror Museum

10 Budapest Zoo

MAP E2 ▪ XIV, Városliget, Állatkerti körút 6–12 ▪ 06 1 273 49 00 ▪ Open May–Aug: 9am–6pm Mon–Fri, 9am–7pm Sat & Sun; Sep: 9am–5:30pm Mon–Fri, 9am–6pm Sat & Sun; Nov–Feb: 9am–4pm daily; Mar & Oct: 9am–5pm Mon–Fri, 9am–5:30pm Sat & Sun ▪ Adm ▪ www.zoobudapest.com

Established in 1866, the city's zoo is one of the best in Central Europe, and is known for its large primate house. Other highlights include a huge reptile house and an enclosed butterfly garden with more than 100 species. The animal enclosures mostly mimic their natural habitat. The zoo's animal houses are listed buildings, built in late Secessionist style between 1909 and 1911.

A DAY IN CITY PARK

▶ MORNING

Városliget is a great place for a family outing. Start off early with a dip in Budapest's most popular thermal baths, **Széchenyi** *(see p95)*, situated right in the middle of City Park with its own metro station on the Lilliputian Millennium line. Refreshed, you can then take the kids next door to the **Budapest Zoo**, to admire both animals and buildings. You can get information about the programmes for the day at the entrance. After the trip to the zoo, take a walk around the park's lake at Kós Károly sétány. After the stroll, head to Turkish coffee house **Café Kara** *(see p98)* at Andrassy Avenue for fresh coffee and delectable sandwiches.

AFTERNOON

Start the afternoon off at the **Museum of Fine Arts** *(see p95)* at the edge of the park in **Heroes' Square**. Although you could spend all afternoon here, try to restrict yourself to an hour and a half, but don't miss the Raphael *Madonna* or the collection of El Grecos. Then take the kids for a ride on the historic M1 metro line between Heroes' Square and the **Oktogon**; they'll love the bright-yellow trains. Afterwards, head back to the park to admire the architecture of **Vajdahunyad Castle**, ideally from a rowing boat on the park's central lake. If you are visiting in winter, you can go ice-skating on the lake *(see p53)*. Finally, end the day with a superb family dinner at **Robinson** *(see p99)*, one of Budapest's most famous restaurants.

See map on p94 ←

Cafés and Pubs

Elegant Art Deco-style interior at the New York Café és Étterem

1 New York Café és Étterem

MAP D4 ▪ VII, Erzsébet körút 9–11 ▪ 06 1 322 38 49 ▪ Open 8am–10pm daily ▪ www.newyorkcafe.hu

Sip hot chocolate or a martini at this lavish Budapest institution (see p57).

2 Mirage Café & Bar

MAP E2 ▪ VI, Dózsa György út 88 ▪ 06 1 462 70 70 ▪ Open 10am–10pm daily

The location opposite Heroes' Square pulls in the crowds, but the food and prices are good for a tourist hotspot.

3 Kaledonia

MAP M1 ▪ VI, Mozsár utca 9 ▪ 06 1 311 76 11 ▪ Open 2pm–midnight Mon–Fri, noon–midnight Sat & Sun

This Scottish pub serves hearty meals. Great place to watch sporting events.

4 Menza

MAP M2 ▪ VI, Liszt Ferenc tér 2 ▪ 06 1 413 14 82 ▪ Open 11am–11pm daily ▪ www.menzaetterem.hu

Restaurant and coffee house with a retro design and a modern take on Magyar canteen favourites.

5 Café Vian

MAP M2 ▪ VI, Liszt Ferenc tér 9 ▪ Open 9am–1am daily ▪ www.cafe vian.com

Coffee, cocktails, pasta and salads make Vian (see p57) a one-stop shop.

6 Sugar Shop

MAP M2 ▪ Paulay Ede utca 48 ▪ 06 1 321 66 72 ▪ Open 11am–7pm daily ▪ www.sugarshop.hu

Give in to the irresistible, colourful sweets at this confectionery and candy shop. Tejberizs (milk rice pudding) is a local favourite.

7 Ferdinand Monarchy Czech Beerhouse

MAP D2 ▪ Szív út 30 ▪ 06 1 312 20 77 ▪ Open noon–11pm daily

Reminiscent of Prague, serving speciality beers from the Czech Republic.

8 Flow

MAP D3 ▪ VI, Andrássy út 66 ▪ Open 9am–7pm daily ▪ www. flowcoffee.hu

Come here for coffee and tea from around the world, and a menu that is a treat for vegans and vegetarians.

9 Café Kara

MAP E2 ▪ VI, Andrássy út 130 ▪ 06 1 269 41 35 ▪ Open 10am–10pm daily

Turkish-style coffee and beer house with a range of cocktails. Dog friendly.

10 Két Szerecsen

MAP D3 ▪ Nagymező utca 14 ▪ Open 9am–midnight daily ▪ www. ketszerecsen.hu

This bistro has excellent food, coffee and an extensive wine menu.

Restaurants

PRICE CATEGORIES
For a three-course meal for one, with half a bottle of wine (or equivalent meal), taxes and extra charges.

F under Ft5,000 **FF** Ft5,000–10,000
FFF over Ft10,000

1 Gundel
MAP E2 ■ Gundel Károly út 4 ■ 06 1 889 81 11 ■ Open 9am–10pm Wed–Sat ■ www.gundel.hu ■ FFF
Probably Hungary's most famous restaurant and one of the priciest. Traditional yet creative food.

2 Király100
MAP D3 ■ VI, Király utca 100 ■ 06 1 351 67 93 ■ Open 11am–11pm daily ■ www.kiraly100.hu ■ FFF
This bistro serves amazing steaks, and offers a vast selection of *palinka* (Hungarian fruit brandy).

3 The Big Fish
MAP D3 ■ VI, Andrássy út 44 ■ 06 1 269 06 93 ■ Open noon–10pm daily ■ www.thebigfish.hu ■ FFF
Pick what you like from the extensive fresh seafood counter and have it cooked just as you wish.

The Big Fish seafood counter

4 Porto di Pest
MAP M2 ■ VI, Liszt Ferenc tér 3 ■ 06 1 351 87 38 ■ Open 11am–midnight Mon–Sat (to 11pm Sun) ■ FF
One of the few places on Liszt Ferenc tér that attracts more locals than tourists, Porto di Pest serves delicious goulash, burgers and local beers.

5 Bagolyvár
MAP E2 ■ XIV, Gundel Károly út 2 ■ 06 1 468 31 10 ■ Open noon–11pm daily ■ www.bagolyvar.com ■ FF
A family-friendly restaurant serving traditional Hungarian food is set in an atmospheric dark-beamed villa.

6 Maharaja
MAP D3 ■ VII, Csengery utca 24 ■ 06 1 250 75 44 ■ Open noon–11pm daily ■ FF
Family-run Maharaja presents subtly spiced, mouthwatering curries.

7 Trattoria Gusto
MAP M2 ■ VI, Liszt Ferenc tér 11 ■ 06 1 321 84 25 ■ Open noon–11pm daily ■ FF
Clay-oven pizzas and other Italian delicacies served in a pretty dining room.

8 Arriba Taqueria
MAP D3 ■ VI, Teréz körút 25 ■ 06 30 490 88 96 ■ Open 11am–10pm daily ■ F
Although essentially just fast food, served at the counter, this is the best Tex-Mex eatery in Budapest.

9 Robinson
MAP E2 ■ XIV, Városligeti-tó ■ Open noon–4pm & 6–11pm daily ■ www.robinsonrestaurant.hu ■ FF
Located on a tiny island, this place serves seafood in an informal setting.

10 Parázs Presszo Thai Restaurant
MAP D3 ■ Jókai utca 8 ■ Open noon–10pm daily ■ www.parazspresszo.com ■ FF
A small restaurant perfect for lovers of spicy Thai food.

See map on p94

🔟 Greater Budapest

While the city centre has enough to keep most visitors happy for weeks, Budapest's suburbs have now spread out into the surrounding Pannonian plains and incorporate some extraordinary sights. These include the former Roman city of Aquincum, today bordered by a train line and a highway, as well as the former Roman garrison at Óbuda to the southwest. The Buda Hills, once some distance from the city, now have villas and apartment blocks in their foothills, while the remarkable limestone caves at Pálvölgy and Szemlő-hegy are almost lost in the city's urban sprawl.

Worker's Movement Memorial, Memento Park

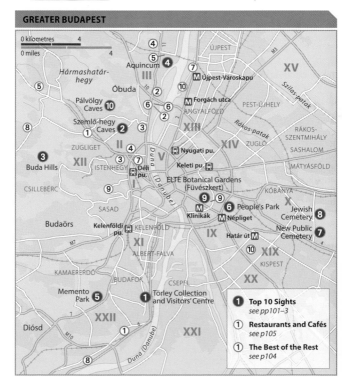

GREATER BUDAPEST

0 kilometres   4
0 miles   4

① **Top 10 Sights**
see pp101–3

① **Restaurants and Cafés**
see p105

① **The Best of the Rest**
see p104

1 Törley Collection and Visitors' Centre

MAP P3 ■ XXII, Anna utca 5–7
■ 06 1 339 23 00 ■ By appointment only ■ www.torleymuzeum.hu

Widely recognized as the father of the Hungarian wine industry, József Törley studied wine-making in Reims, the Champagne capital of France. He returned to Hungary in the 1880s, and set about producing superb sparkling wine in Budafok, a Budapest suburb. The Törley Collection displays the long and tumultuous history of Törley sparkling wines. With clear Ottoman influences, the architecture is also a major highlight of the centre.

Törley Collection exhibition

2 Szemlő-hegy Caves

MAP N1 ■ II, Pusztaszeri út 35
■ 06 1 325 60 01 ■ By appointment only ■ Adm ■ www.dunaipoly.hu

Known to many as the city of thermal waters, Budapest is also known for its caves. North of the city centre are the Pilis Hills, home to several fabulous cave systems. The Szemlő-hegy Caves are the closest to the city, on bus route No. 11 from Batthyány Square (Batthyány tér) to Pusztaszeri út (it's about a mile walk from there). The caves feature splendid formations known as cave pearls that resemble bunches of grapes growing out of the rock. These are produced by the action of hot springs penetrating limestone. The air here is said to be therapeutic for bronchial infections.

3 Buda Hills

MAP N1

The forested Buda Hills to the west of the city make an ideal getaway (see p103). The best way to reach them is to take the Cogwheel Railway (see p52), which begins at Városmajor. At the top, a short walk leads to the huge TV tower. The Children's Railway (see p52) begins at the base of the tower and meanders through the Buda Hills to its terminus at Hűvös Valley. En route is the Elizabeth Lookout Tower (Erzsébet-kilátó), which has a chairlift that takes you back to Buda. It was constructed by Frigyes Schulek in 1910, but the purpose for which it was built remains a mystery.

4 Aquincum

MAP P1 ■ III, Szentendrei út 139 ■ 06 250 16 50 ■ Open Apr–Oct: 9am–6pm Tue–Sun; Nov–Mar: 10am–4pm Tue–Sun ■ Adm ■ aquincum.hu

The capital of the Roman province of Pannonia, Aquincum was for centuries the largest city in Central Europe. Excavated in the 19th century, it is one of the city's most popular sights. The outlines of streets and buildings are clearly visible. The museum, inside a Neo-Classical Lapidarium, houses Roman artifacts found at the site and models showing what the town once looked like.

Exterior of Aquincum Museum

Sculpture in Memento Park

5 Memento Park
MAP N3 ■ XXII, Balatoni út
■ 06 1 424 75 00 ■ Open 10am–6pm
daily ■ Adm ■ www.mementopark.hu

The grounds of Memento Park bring together over 40 examples of the Communist-era statues and placques (some astonishingly huge) that once stood in public spaces all over Budapest. Marx, Engels and Lenin are all present, as is the Stalin pedestal, complete with a full-scale replica of his boots: these were all that remained when Stalin's statue was toppled and destroyed during the 1956 revolution. There's also a Trabant – known as "the people's car" – on show, while multimedia displays in a barracks-style building reveal some of the methods the AVH, the Hungarian secret police, used to spy on their own people. There are buses to the park from Deák tér at 11:45am each day.

6 People's Park
MAP P2 ■ VIII, Népliget

The city's largest park, Népliget was laid out in the 1860s and covers an area of 112 ha (277 acres). It has large tracts of grass and trees, as well as flower beds and playgrounds. Népliget was also the site of the city's first motor racing track, and even hosted a Grand Prix in 1936, when Tazio Nuvolari won in his Alfa Romeo. The track fell into disuse after 1972 and, when Hungary decided to host Formula One in the 1980s, a new track, Hungaroring, was built outside town.

7 New Public Cemetery
MAP Q2 ■ X, Kozma utca 8–10
■ 06 1 433 73 56 ■ Visitor's centre:
10am–4pm Tue–Thu; cemetery:
7am–5pm daily (to 5:30pm Mar, to
7pm Apr, to 8pm May–Jul, to 7pm
Aug, to 6pm Sep)

This peaceful cemetery, found to the southwest of Pest, is one of the largest in Europe. It is an expansive burial site and the resting place of around 1.5 million Hungarians, including Imre Nagy *(see p41)* and other participants of the 1956 Revolution. Their graves are found in plots 300 and 301, close to which there is a visitor's centre that shows a series of short films chronicling the lives of some those buried here.

8 Jewish Cemetery
MAP Q2 ■ XVII, Kozma utca
■ Open 8am–3pm Sun–Fri (summer:
to 4pm) ■ www.budapestjewish
cemetery.com

Opened in 1893 and full of elaborate tombs, this cemetery is a stark reminder of the wealth and influence

---

THE MARVELLOUS MAGYARS

In the 1950s Hungary had the most gifted football team in the world. In November 1953, the team achieved a legendary 6-3 win over England at Wembley Stadium (below), which was trumped by an even more impressive 7-1 victory in Budapest a year later. The English press dubbed them the "Marvellous Magyars", and the star player, Ferenc Puskás, the "Galloping Major", as he was once a major in the Hungarian army. Puskás fled Hungary in 1956; defecting to Spain, he led Real Madrid to three of their five European Cup triumphs.

wielded by Budapest's Jews before World War II. Some of the tombs were designed by leading architects, including Ödön Lechner and Gyula Fodor.

⑨ ELTE Botanical Garden (Füvészkert)

MAP F6 ▪ VIII, Illés utca 25 ▪ 06 1 210 10 74 ▪ Open Nov–Mar: 9am–4pm daily; Apr–Oct: 10am–5pm daily ▪ Adm

Spread over 3 ha (8 acres) in eastern Budapest, the ELTE Botanical Garden offers relief from the bustle of the city centre. The gardens are part of ELTE University, though they were first laid out by the Festetics family, who lived in the Neo-Classical villa that is now the administration centre. They are renowned for their palm trees.

Visitors admire the Pálvölgy Caves

⑩ Pálvölgy Caves

MAP N1 ▪ II, Szépvölgyi út 162 ▪ 06 1 325 95 05 ▪ By appointment only ▪ Adm ▪ No children under 5 ▪ www.dunaipoly.hu

A hut at the foot of a steep cliff marks the entrance to the Pálvölgy Caves. As well as the cave pearl formations that are also found in Szemlő-hegy, Pálvölgy is known for its formations that are said to resemble animals. Though many of the caves are accessible, and can be visited via stairs, several of the more spectacular formations can only be seen by joining a guided tour. Wear warm clothes as the temperatures inside can be chilly.

A DAY IN THE BUDA HILLS

▶ MORNING

Start the day by taking bus No. 291 from Nyugati Pu to its terminus at the foot of the Libegő (chairlift), which gently takes you up to the summit of **János Hill**. From here, it is a short walk to the **Children's Railway** *(see p52)*, a splendid relic of Hungary's Communist past. As the train meanders through the hills, you can stop off and climb to the top of the extraordinary **Elizabeth Lookout Tower** *(see p101)* for sensational views of the city below. Then take the steam train, which leaves on the hour throughout summer. Get off at **Szépjuhászné Station** and try the station's super outdoor café for lunch.

AFTERNOON

Set off on a well-marked path to the **Budakeszi Wildlife Park** *(0623 45 17 83; www.vadaspark-budakeszi.hu)*. Occupying an area of 327 ha (808 acres), it has a wide variety of animals to see, from wild boars – which also roam freely in the surrounding countryside – to packs of wolves. There is also a separate reserve for plantlife. Take the park's walking safari tour to visit its best sections and enjoy climbing in the adventure park. The park's own restaurant is a great place for dinner, serving generous amounts of traditional local food and Hungarian wine, and there is lively folk music and dancing every evening after 6pm. As the Children's Railway will almost certainly be closed by the time you finish eating, you can take bus No. 22 to **Széll Kálmán tér**. From there, you can get the metro back to the centre of the city.

See map on p100 ←

The Best of the Rest

1 Tropicarium-Oceanarium

MAP N3 ■ XXII, Nagytétényi út 37–43 ■ 06 1 424 30 53 ■ Open 10am–8pm daily ■ Adm ■ www.tropicarium.hu

You can stare into the eyes of a shark or glimpse an alligator at this aquarium and indoor tropical rainforest.

Displays at the Kassák Museum

2 Kassák Museum

MAP P1 ■ III, Fő tér 1 ■ 06 368 70 21 ■ Open 10am–5pm Wed–Sun ■ Adm ■ www.kassakmuzeum.hu

Housed in Zichy Palace, this museum showcases the works of avant-garde artist Lajos Kassák.

3 Óbuda Amphitheatre

MAP N1 ■ III, Bécsi út

Dating from around AD 140–150, the military amphitheatre is the larger of Budapest's two Roman amphitheatres, and still has two arched entrances as well as tunnels from where wild animals entered.

4 Aquincum Amphitheatre

MAP P1 ■ III, Szentendrei út

Once packed with 10,000 spectators, Aquincum's civil amphitheatre (see p101) lies sandwiched between the HÉV railway and a main road. It was built around AD 250–300.

5 Aqueduct

MAP P1 ■ III, Szentendrei út

A restored section of the 2nd-century aqueduct that carried water from Óbuda to Aquincum lies to the east of Szentendrei út. Traffic runs along either side, so take care.

6 Hungarian Museum of Trade and Tourism

MAP P1 ■ III, Korona tér 1 ■ 06 1 375 62 49 ■ Open 10am–7pm Tue–Sun ■ Adm ■ www.mkvm.hu

Explore the history of Hungarian catering and home cuisine, and learn to cook some traditional dishes.

7 Hospital in the Rock Nuclear Bunker Museum

MAP N2 ■ I, Lovas út 4/c ■ Open 10am–7pm daily ■ Adm ■ www.sziklakorhaz.eu

Wax figures bring to life the eerie history of the system of caverns under Buda Castle, an emergency hospital and shelter from World War II that became a nuclear bunker by 1962.

8 Nagytétény Palace

MAP N3 ■ XXII, Kastélypark utca 9–11 ■ Closed for renovation

A design museum featuring classic furniture, housed in one of Hungary's best Baroque palaces.

9 Ludovika Academy

MAP P2 ■ X, Ludovika tér 2–6 ■ 06 1 210 10 85 ■ Open 10am–5pm Wed–Mon ■ Adm ■ www.nhmus.hu

Part of this former military school is home to the Natural History Museum.

10 Wekerle Estate

MAP P2 ■ XIX, Kós Károly tér

Central Europe's first Garden City was inspired by Transylvania's Saxon villages. Homes here are sought after.

Home on the Wekerle Estate

Restaurants and Cafés

PRICE CATEGORIES
For a three-course meal for one, with half a bottle of wine (or equivalent meal), taxes and extra charges.

F under Ft5,000   **FF** Ft5,000–10,000
FFF over Ft10,000

1 Remiz
MAP N1 ■ II, Budakeszi út 5
■ Open noon–11pm Mon–Sat, noon–5pm Sun ■ FFF ■ www.remiz.hu
Good Hungarian food and wine, plus Budapest's best rack of ribs. There's also a lovely garden.

2 Kéhli
MAP P1 ■ III, Mókus utca 22
■ Open noon–10pm Mon–Fri & Sun (to 10:30pm Sat) ■ FF ■ www.kehli.hu
Founded in 1899, Kéhli serves good old-fashioned Hungarian food, with a live folk band that plays most nights.

3 Fióka
MAP N2 ■ XII, Városmajor utca 75 ■ Open 11am–midnight daily ■ FF ■ www.fiokaetterem.hu
This charming gastropub serves lots of game and very good local wines.

4 Auguszt 1870 Patisserie
MAP A3 ■ II, Fény u. 8 ■ 06 1 316 38 17 ■ Open 10am–6pm Tue–Sat ■ FFF ■ www.auguszt1870.hu
Serving traditional Hungarian and French inspired pastries since 1870, this patisserie is a local favourite.

5 Náncsi Néni
MAP N1 ■ II, Ördögárok út 80
■ Open noon–11pm daily ■ F ■ www.nancsineni.hu
Fantastic regional dishes that only use farm-fresh ingredients.

6 Zöld Kapu Vendéglő
MAP P1 ■ III, Szőlő utca 42
■ Open 10am–10pm daily ■ FF ■ www.zoldkapuvendeglo.hu
A traditional Hungarian restaurant with a garden, serving huge portions of hearty food in the middle of Óbuda.

7 Központ Bisztró
MAP P1 ■ IV, Szent István tér 1
■ 0620 374 97 85 ■ Open 8am–10pm Mon–Fri, 10am–10pm Sat & Sun ■ F ■ www.kozpontbisztro.hu
Popular with the locals for its burgers and international cuisine.

Interior of Budai Gesztenyés

8 Budai Gesztenyés
MAP N2 ■ Budakeszi, Fő utca 1
■ 0623 45 05 34 ■ Open 11am–11pm daily ■ FF ■ www.budaigesztenyes.hu
Modern European food with a Hungarian twist. There are just a few options for each course. Given the high quality, prices are a steal.

9 Jardinette
MAP N2 ■ XII, Némétvölgyi út 136 ■ Open noon–10pm Tue–Thu, 9am–10pm Fri & Sat, 9am–8pm Sun ■ FF ■ www.jardinette.hu
Exquisite French food served in a lovely garden. The wine list is superb.

10 Eat & Meet
MAP P1 ■ XIII, Danubius utca 14 ■ Open 6:30–10pm daily ■ FF ■ www.eatmeet-hungary.com
A local family serves dinner in their apartment overlooking the Danube. Traditional Hungarian dishes are paired with local wines, and your hosts teach you about their country's cuisine, history and culture.

See map on p100

Streetsmart

**Picturesque buildings in the
Castle Hill district of Buda**

Getting Around

Arriving by Air

All flights to Budapest arrive at **Liszt Ferenc International Airport**. It has connections to cities in the UK and most other major European cities, as well as transatlantic flights to New York.

Bus line 200E operates between Terminal 2 and Budapest's Nagyvárad tér and Népliget metro stations 24-hours a day. The bus also stops at Ferihegy vasútállomás, the airport's train station, from where more than 100 trains per day provide easy access to the city centre. Taxis can be ordered at the **Főtaxi** booths located at the exits. **MiniBud** offers a minibus service to major hotels for a flat fee.

Arriving by Train

The train is a great way to reach Budapest. The city's main station, Keleti, is close to the centre and is served by direct trains from most major central European cities. You can buy tickets and passes for multiple international journeys via **Eurail** or **Interrail**. All trains within Hungary are run by **MÁV** (Magyar Ilamvasutak). Fast InterCity services in Hungary link the capital with Debrecen, Szeged, Pécs and Győr, stopping only at major towns and cities. There are a number of other services, but they are slower and make more stops. Prices for all trains are relatively cheap. Tickets can be bought from stations or online from MÁV.

Arriving by Road

All international coaches arrive at Népliget Bus Station in southern Pest, which is close to Népliget metro station on line M3.

There are no border checks for vehicles entering Hungary from Austria, Slovakia or Slovenia. There are, however, for those entering from Croatia, Romania or Ukraine; during peak season and public holidays, queues can be long. Budapest is at the centre of Hungary's extensive network of motorways and can be reached quickly from all border crossing points.

Public Transport

Budapest has an extensive public transport network made up of bus, trolleybus, tram and metro services. All services are operated by Budapesti Közlekedési Központ, or **BKK**. Safety and hygiene measures, timetables, ticket information, transport maps and more can be obtained from the BKK website.

Tickets

BKK runs an information centre at the airport where you can buy single tickets and longer-term travelcards. These can also be bought from self-service machines at metro stations, newsagents, and major bus and tram stops. Single tickets can be purchased from the driver on buses and trams, but cost an extra 100 Hungarian forint. The self-service machines take cards, but if purchasing a ticket on board a tram or bus you will need to have the exact amount in cash. Single tickets need to be franked on board buses, trolleybuses and trams, and at the entrance to metro stations.

Metro

Budapest has four metro lines, most easily distinguished by their colours: yellow (M1), red (M2), blue (M3) and green (M4). Three lines (M1, M2 and M3) intersect at Deák Ferenc tér station, while the M4 line intersects with the M2 at Keleti pályaudvar and with the M3 at Kálvin tér. Services run from 4:30am until 11:30pm. Remember to validate your ticket at the machines located at the station entrances.

Bus and Trolleybus

Budapest has around 200 different bus routes, as well as 15 trolleybus routes that run only in Pest. Daytime services run from about 4:30am to 11:30pm, with departures on most routes every 10–20 minutes. There is a good range of night buses operating across the city every 15–60 minutes. Departure times and a list of destinations are on display at each stop. Tickets must be punched upon entering the bus.

Tram

There are more than 30 tram lines in Budapest. They serve almost every part of the city except the hilly parts of Buda. Trams are yellow and are a good way of sightseeing in the centre. Services start early in the morning, from about 4:30am, and run regularly until 11pm or midnight, depending on the route. Night trams operate only on line 6, every 10–15 minutes. Validate your ticket in the machine inside the tram. All stops display the relevant tram numbers and the timetable. BKK tickets and passes are valid right along the line.

Boats

Budapest has three public boat lines, the D-11, D-12 and D-14. Boats are great for sightseeing and many stops are located near famous sights, such as Parliament. In general, boats operate every 30–60 minutes between 6:30am and 8:30pm; however, timetables are seasonal. Tickets can be purchased on-board or at a pier. Passes and travelcards are valid during the week, but you need a special ticket at weekends or if you do not have a pass or a travelcard.

A number of companies offer tours of the Danube by boat, with tours covering different sights and distances. **Cityrama** runs a short, one-hour boat tour which is a good introduction to the city's history (and the Danube's role in it), while **Silverline Cruises** operates a number of longer trips, many offering food, drinks and entertainment.

Driving

This is the least convenient method of getting around Budapest. There are very few places to park (almost none at all in the city centre), traffic can be busy during the week and one-way systems can be tricky to navigate. If you do decide to drive, then a wide variety of car-hire firms, such as Hertz and Avis, can be found at the airport.

Taxi

Taxi ranks are located throughout Budapest and taxis can also be hailed on the street, but to avoid inflated fares book from your hotel or by phone. Reputable companies include **City Taxi** and Főtaxi. Ridesharing services such as Uber are banned in Hungary.

Cycling

Cycling in Budapest is often difficult and fairly dangerous. Cyclists have to be very careful of the tram rails and the uneven, cobblestoned surfaces of some roads. However, Budapest's main roads are usually open to cyclists and designated cycle lanes are available on a growing number of roads. The provision of cycle routes in the city and the opening of one-way streets to contraflow cycling (indicated by signs allowing this) have led to cycling becoming increasingly popular.

Bikebase hire out bikes and are a good source of information about bicycle routes in the city. The **MOL Bubi** public bike-sharing scheme is another way of cycling around Budapest. It consists of nearly 150 docking stations and 1,900 bicycles found at several locations in the city.

Walking

Budapest is a great city for those who want to explore on foot. A host of pedestrian-friendly measures have been implemented in recent years to reduce the number of cars using the city centre's streets. Váci Street and Vörösmarty Square are car-free, as are many of the streets around the Royal Palace. The main avenues, especially Andrássy út, have wide pavements perfect for strolling, while City Park and Margaret Island are great for longer walks.

Practical Information

Passports and Visas

For entry requirements, including visas, consult your nearest Hungarian embassy or check the Hungarian foreign ministry's **Consular Services** website. EU nationals and citizens of the UK, US, Canada, Australia and New Zealand do not need visas for stays of up to three months, providing they have a valid passport. Citizens of all other countries should check entry requirements from the Consular Services website before travelling.

Most countries have consular representation in Hungary, including the UK and the US.

Government Advice

Now more than ever, it is important to consult both your and the Hungarian government's advice before travelling. The **UK Foreign and Commonwealth Office**, **US Department of State**, **Australian Department of Foreign Affairs and Trade** and **Hungarian Police** offer the latest information on security, health and local regulations.

Customs Information

You can find information on the laws relating to goods and currency taken in or out of Hungary on the **National Tax and Customs Administration** (NAV) website.

If arriving from outside the EU, besides personal belongings you can bring the following items into the country – 40 cigarettes, four litres of wine, one litre of spirits and €300 worth of gifts. There are no limits on the import of goods from EU countries.

Insurance

We recommend taking out a comprehensive insurance policy covering theft, loss of belongings, medical care, cancellations and delays, and read the small print carefully.

Health

Hungary has a good healthcare system. Emergency medical care in Hungary is free for all UK and EU citizens, providing they have either an EHIC (European Health Insurance Card) or a **GHIC** (UK Global Health Insurance Card). Make sure to present this card as soon as possible when receiving emergency medical treatment. You may have to pay after treatment and reclaim the money later. For other visitors, payment of medical expenses is the patient's responsibility. It is therefore important to arrange comprehensive medical insurance before travelling.

For information regarding COVID-19 vaccination requirements, consult government advice. No other vaccinations are required for visitors to Hungary.

Unless stated otherwise, tap water in both Budapest and the surrounding area is safe to drink.

Pharmacies are well stocked and ubiquitous: most open seven days a week. The Hungarian for pharmacy is *patika* or *gyógyszertár*, although you will see the German word *apotheke* in use as well. In the case of a minor ailment, the chemist will be able to recommend a suitable treatment. Some drugs require a prescription, while others can be sold over the counter in pharmacies. If your nearest pharmacy is closed, there should be a list displayed on the door or in the window of all the local chemists – it will indicate which ones are on 24-hour emergency duty. The 24-hour pharmacies closest to the city centre are Déli Gyógyszertár, opposite Déli Station in Buda, and Teréz Patika, near Oktogon metro station in Pest.

Not all medical staff will speak English. In an emergency, either call an ambulance or visit **Péterfy Kórház-Rendelőintézet**, the city's most central 24-hour emergency room, located close to Keleti station. There are a number of private clinics with English-speaking staff and a higher standard of care, but these are expensive and neither EHIC or GHIC are accepted. The most central is **Medoc Klinika**.

Hungarian dental treatment is good and cheap. If you urgently need a dentist, call **Smilistic**

Dental Services, which operates Monday to Friday.

Smoking, Alcohol and Drugs

Hungary has some of the EU's toughest anti-smoking legislation and smoking is banned in all indoor public spaces, including on public transport and in stations. Even when outside, smokers must be five metres from a building entrance before lighting up. Cigarettes can only be purchased from branches of the national chain of tobacco shops (Nemzeti Dohánybolt).

It is illegal to drive in Hungary after consuming any alcohol. If your blood alcohol level is above 0 per cent but under 0.08 per cent you will be fined; if it is over 0.08 per cent you will be subject to legal proceedings.

Hungary has a zero-tolerance anti-drugs policy, and possession of even the smallest amounts of illegal substances can land you with a large fine or a even prison sentence.

ID

By law in Hungary, you need to carry your passport or national ID card with you at all times and present it to the police if asked to do so. You will be asked to present ID when checking in to accommodation, including private apartment rentals.

Personal Security

Budapest is one of the safest capital cities in Europe, but it is always a good idea to take sensible precautions when wandering around the city, especially at night. Extra precaution should be taken against pickpockets, particularly on busy public transport routes and in popular tourist areas – in particular in and around Váci Street. Rental vehicles can be targeted by thieves, so ensure no valuables are left inside the car. It is also a good idea not to take valuables to the city's thermal baths, as thieves may occasionally target lockers.

If you have anything stolen, report the crime as soon as possible at the nearest police station and take ID with you. Get a copy of the crime report to claim on your insurance. Contact your embassy or consulate if your passport is lost or stolen, or in the event of a serious crime or accident.

Hungary is a largely conservative society, with the result that LGBTQ+ communities are not always met with acceptance. While same-sex civil partnerships have been legal in Hungary since 2009, same-sex marriage is banned by the constitution. In 2021, Hungary's government passed legislation barring people from changing their gender on official documents, and banning schools from discussing LGBTQ+ topics. Budapest itself, however, is more welcoming. The city has good LGBTQ+ friendly nightlife and hosts an annual, month-long Pride festival every June, which includes film screenings, plays and parties, as well as a huge Pride parade. If you do feel unsafe, the **Safe Space Alliance** pinpoints your nearest place of refuge.

The **emergency services** (fire, police and ambulance) can be contacted by dialling 112. Few police officers speak English but all are happy to help tourists. The Hungarian word for police is rendőrség.

Travellers with Specific Requirements

Many of Budapest's attractions are located in areas with cobbled streets, steep slopes, steps or narrow pavements, presenting difficulties for visitors with limited mobility; this is particularly true of sights in the Castle Hill area. Historic buildings often lack lifts or ramps, but larger hotels, restaurants and bars are now obliged to have accessible, well-equipped bedrooms and bathrooms.

Newer trams and buses, and most metro stations offer step-free access. **BKV** (Budapesti Közlekedési Zrt.) offers a door-to-door bus service.

The Hungarian Federation of Disabled Persons' Associations, more commonly known as **MEOSZ**, has a useful website with information on disabled access in Budapest – although currently only in Hungarian.

Time Zone

Budapest uses Central European time, in keeping with the majority of mainland Europe. This means it is two hours ahead of Greenwich Mean Time (GMT) in the summer and one hour ahead in winter.

Money

Hungary's currency is the Forint (Ft). Major credit and debit cards are accepted everywhere and contactless payments are increasingly common. Minimum amounts are often required for card transactions, however,

so carry cash for smaller payments. ATMs (bank-automata) are available outside banks, which are ubiquitous, as well as some shops.

It is customary to tip waiters 10 per cent of the bill, hotel housekeeping Ft200 per day and concierge staff Ft200–400.

Electrical Appliances

The electric current is 220 volts. Many electrical appliances, such as mobile and laptop chargers, have 110/220V transformers built in, so converters may be less of a concern, especially if you are coming from North America. Bring European adaptors with two round pins.

Mobile Phones and Wi-Fi

Visitors travelling to Hungary with EU call plans can use their devices abroad without being affected by data roaming charges. Other visitors can buy a local SIM card in order to take advantage of local rates. Ask your home carrier for the unlock code to use a different SIM card. Telenor, Vodafone and Telekom, the three big Hungarian mobile networks, offer pre-paid SIM cards, sold at most newsstands, kiosks and mobile phone stores.

Budapest is well covered with Wi-Fi hotspots. Cafés and restaurants are usually happy to permit the use of their Wi-Fi on the condition that you make a purchase. Wi-Fi is now almost always free in hotels. Lizst Ference International Airport also

has free Wi-Fi. The app **WiFi Map** lists most free Wi-Fi spots in the city.

Postal Services

Hungarian mail is fast and reliable. Offices of Magyar Posta, the national mail service, usually open 7am–6pm. You can buy stamps from the post office and newsstands. A standard letter weighing up to 20g or a postcard costs Ft370 within the EU, Ft435 to other destinations. Most Hungarian post offices offer mail-holding (poste restante) services

Opening Hours

Banks are generally open 9am–4pm on weekdays, though opening hours can vary significantly. Shops keep long hours from Monday to Saturday (often 10am–8pm), with malls staying open until 10pm. Many shops, mainly the larger ones, are also open on Sundays, but they might close earlier than on other days. You should find plenty of small kiosks and a few hypermarkets selling basic necessities open 24 hours a day throughout the city.

Most museums and other main attractions are open every day, although some are shut on Mondays.

COVID-19 Increased rates of infection may result in temporary opening hours and/or closures. Always check ahead before visiting museums, attractions and hospitality venues.

Weather

Budapest's climate is one of extremes. Summers can be very hot, with temperatures soaring above 30°C (86°F) in July and August, while winter is bitterly cold, and snow not uncommon. Spring is wet: May and June are the months with the heaviest rainfall. Late summer and autumn are perhaps the best times to visit the city.

Visitor Information

Budapest Info, the city's official tourist organization, has an excellent website that contains useful information for tourists; it also runs several **Tourinform** centres in Budapest. The main office is on Deák tér, and there are others at Liszt Ferenc tér, Buda Castle and the airport. They organize tours and provide general information. **Visit Hungary**, the Hungarian Tourism Agency's official website and app, is very good for planning excursions outside of Budapest. **Pink Budapest**, meanwhile, has up-to-date recommendations on LGBTQ+ friendly venues and events.

The **We Love Budapest** website is an excellent independent source of events listings, as is the free monthly **Funzine Budapest** magazine and website. Look out for City Walks maps: these practical and informative maps help you explore the city's major attractions over 2- or 3-hour walking tours. They are updated every month and are available for free in most hotels.

The Budapest Card entitles a visitor to use most city transport free of charge, and provides discounted or free entry to some museums. It also entitles you to a discount on tickets to a number of selected spas, restaurants and many cultural events. Purchase it online via the Budapest Info website, at official tourist information centres, or at the Liszt Ferenc International Airport.

Visiting Churches and Cathedrals

When visiting churches and religious sites, visitors should dress respectfully. Make sure you cover your torso, upper arms and knees.

Language

Hungarian, or Magyar, is the official language in Hungary. English is widely spoken in Budapest by people working in the services industry.

Taxes and Refunds

The price of all goods in Hungary includes a value-added tax of 27 per cent (ÁFA). With the exception of antiques and works of art, it is possible for non-EU residents to claim back this tax on anything costing more than Ft50,000. However, before buying expensive goods with the intention of reclaiming the VAT, it is advisable to consult the vendor about whether they have the necessary VAT-reclaim form. When leaving the country, present these papers with the receipt and your ID at customs to receive your refund.

Accommodation

Budapest has a broad range of places to stay, including a number of luxury hotels housed in 19th-century palaces.

During the peak summer season – which runs from June to September – and at Christmas and New Year, lodgings fill up and prices become inflated, so book in advance. A resort tax is included in the price of a room (resort tax is charged because the city is classed as a health resort). Under Hungarian law, all accommodation providers are required to register guests with the police and issue a receipt of payment.

DIRECTORY

TRAVELLERS WITH SPECIFIC REQUIREMENTS

MEOSZ
ⓦ meosz.hu

BKV
ⓦ bkv.hu/en/
physically_challenged

MOBILE PHONES AND WI-FI

WiFi Map
ⓦ wifimap.io

VISITOR INFORMATION

Budapest Info
ⓦ budapestinfo.hu

Funzine Budapest
ⓦ funzine.hu

Pink Budapest
ⓦ pinkbudapest.com/

Tourinform
MAP C4 ▪ V, Sütő utca 2 (Deák tér)
Ⓒ 06 1 438 80 80 (24 hrs)

Visit Hungary
ⓦ visithungary.com

We love Budapest
ⓦ welovebudapest.com

Places to Stay

PRICE CATEGORIES
For a standard, double room per night (with breakfast if included), taxes and extra charges.
....
F under Ft15,000   FF Ft15,000–30,000   FFF over Ft30,000

Luxury Hotels

Mamaison Andrássy Boutique Hotel

MAP M2 ▪ VI, Andrássy út 111 ▪ 06 1 462 21 00 ▪ www.mamaison andrassy.com ▪ FF

At the Andrássy, you will find all the elegance you could wish for. A Small Luxury Hotels of the World group member, it is set on the city's classiest boulevard. Rooms are superbly furnished, and it has a great restaurant.

Corinthia Hotel Budapest

MAP D3 ▪ VII, Erzsébet körút 43–9 ▪ 06 1 479 40 00 ▪ www.corinthia.com ▪ FFF

From its faithfully restored Secession façade to the exquisite atriums and foyer, the Grand Royal has been enticing discerning guests since 1896. With its central location, lavish rooms and first-class restaurants, this truly is a fabulous hotel.

Crowne Plaza Budapest

MAP C2 ▪ VIII, Váci út 1-3 ▪ 06 1 288 55 00 ▪ www.ihg.com ▪ FFF

Centrally located next to Nyugati station, this luxury hotel features spacious and well equipped rooms, a magnificent buffet breakfast and a lovely rooftop bar and terrace.

Hilton Budapest

MAP G2 ▪ I, Hess András tér 1–3 ▪ 06 1 889 66 00 ▪ www.hilton.com ▪ FFF

The Hilton Budapest's imposing façade is one of the most instantly recognizable sights in the Castle District. It's a fantastic hotel, with well-furnished rooms, many of which have great Danube views.

Hotel Nemzeti Budapest – MGallery

MAP D4 ▪ VIII, József körút 4 ▪ 06 1 477 45 00 ▪ www.accor.com ▪ FFF

This may be a Neo-Classical building, but the rooms are contemporary. The lobby and common areas are quite stunning, and the wine bar is a lively after-hours hangout.

Kempinski Hotel Corvinus Budapest

MAP L3 ▪ V, Erzsébet tér 7–8 ▪ 06 1 429 37 77 ▪ www.kempinski.com ▪ FFF

While the bold Kempinski Corvinus has a Modernist design on the outside, its interior offers lush furnishings, marble bathrooms and understated luxury. Most rooms overlook Elizabeth Square.

Queen's Court

MAP D4 ▪ VII, Dob utca 63 ▪ 06 1 882 30 00 ▪ www. queenscourthotel budapest.com ▪ FFF

While not particularly attractive from the outside, within the Queen's Court hotel you will find nothing but the best, with the focus on superbly designed suites. It also boasts a luxurious indoor swimming pool and gym.

The Ritz-Carlton, Budapest

MAP L3 ▪ V, Erzsébet tér 9–10 ▪ 06 1 429 55 00 ▪ www.ritzcarlton.com ▪ FFF

A perfect combination of elegance and comfort, the Ritz-Carlton sits in a great location on Elizabeth Square. The listed building has been lovingly furnished in a clean, modern style.

Grand and Historic Hotels

Anantara New York Palace Budapest

MAP D4 ▪ VII, Erzsébet körút 9–11 ▪ 06 1 886 61 11 ▪ www.anantara. com ▪ FFF

At this unashamedly luxurious hotel (see p98), surfaces are rich in marble, bronze, steel and glass, and every en-suite has a marble bathtub. It is also home to the lavish New York Café, one of the great literary hangouts of the 20th century.

Hotel Continental Budapest

MAP M4 ▪ VII, Dohány utca 42–4 ▪ 06 1 815 10 00 ▪ www.continental hotelbudapest.com ▪ FFF

This building, with its stunning Art Nouveau façade, was a large bath house in the 1900s. It is now a business-oriented modern hotel with a roof garden and pool, plus a fitness centre.

Hotel Palazzo Zichy
MAP D5 ■ VIII, Lőrinc pap tér 2 ■ 06 1 235 40 00 ■ www.hotel-palazzo-zichy.hu ■ FFF
This Neo-Baroque mansion, built for Count Zichy, dates from 1899, and is now a luxurious hotel. Superb rooms are of a grand size, and the buffet breakfast is one of the city's best.

Matild Palace
MAP C5 ■ V, Váci utca 36 ■ 06 1 550 50 50 ■ www.marriott.com ■ FFF
First built in 1902, this sumptuous hotel offers palatial accommodation, with elegantly and individually furnished high-ceiling rooms. The loft rooms offer amazing views of central Budapest.

Párisi Udvar Hotel
MAP C5 ■ Petőfi Sándor utca 2-4 ■ 06 1 370 10 00 ■ www.hyatt.com ■ FFF
Part of the Hyatt Group, the Párisi Udvar has brought an Art Nouveau shopping arcade back to life as an opulent hotel. It is decorated with Zsolnay tiles and has a spectacular glass-roofed foyer.

Boutique Hotels

Bohem Art Hotel
MAP L5 ■ V, Molnár utca 35 ■ 06 1 327 90 20 ■ www.bohemarthotel.hu ■ FF
This "art hotel" features the work of local artists. It's superbly located, just metres away from both the river and Váci Street, and room rates are more

than reasonable given the luxurious and stylish nature of the place.

Boutique Hotel Budapest
MAP L5 ■ V, Só utca 6 ■ 06 1 920 21 00 ■ www.boutiquehotelbudapest.com ■ FF
The somewhat minimalist and very contemporary interiors here are as cutting-edge as they come. There is a also a fantastic fusion restaurant.

Brody House
MAP M4 ■ VIII, Bródy Sándor utca 10 ■ 06 1 266 12 11 ■ www.brody.land ■ FF
This boutique hotel is attached to a private members' club. The communal area offers lovely views over the park beside the National Museum, and there is a well-stocked library. The staff are also able to give their visitors a great introduction to the city.

Hotel Parlament
MAP L1 ■ V, Kálmán Imre utca 19 ■ 06 1 374 60 00 ■ www.parlament-hotel.hu ■ FF
Behind its gorgeous exterior, the rooms here are distinguished by their smart wooden floors and simple yet elegant design. There's also a good spa centre, restaurant and bar.

Three Corners Boutique Hotel Bristol
MAP E4 ■ VIII, Kenyérmező utca 4 ■ 06 799 11 00 ■ www.threecorners.com ■ FF
This hotel is spotlessly clean and surprisingly quiet, given its proximity to the railway station.

The staff seem eager to please, and the breakfast buffet is excellent.

Aria Hotel Budapest
MAP L3 ■ V, Hercegprímás utca 5 ■ 06 1 445 40 55 ■ www.ariahotel budapest.com ■ FFF
Part of the exclusive Library Group, the Aria has a musical theme. The elegant interior courtyard here will take your breath away, as will the sublime rooms, all individually designed in quirky styles. Best of all is the rooftop bar, with stunning views.

Mamaison Residence Izabella Budapest
MAP D3 ■ VI, Izabella utca 61 ■ 06 1 475 59 00 ■ www.mamaison izabella.com ■ FFF
An apartment hotel with spacious one-, two- and three-bedroom apartments in a great location, just off Budapest's most exclusive street, Andrássy Avenue. There is a 24-hour reception desk, security, parking and a health club.

Danube View Hotels

Buda Gold
MAP A5 ■ I, Hegyalja út 14 ■ 06 1 209 47 75 ■ www.goldhotel.hu ■ FF
A splendid Buda hotel, located a short walk from the Citadella. Housed in a great building, complete with a tower, it was only built in 1997. Rooms have cherry-wood parquet floors, and most have great views over the Danube or the Buda Hills. The tower rooms, though pricey, are the best.

Hotel Victoria
MAP H2 ▪ I, Bem rakpart 11 ▪ 06 1 457 80 80 ▪ www.victoria.hu ▪ FF
Located beneath Buda Castle on the Danube embankment, this charming, mid-range hotel offers 27 spacious, well-equipped rooms, all with fantastic river views. The staff are knowledge-able and helpful.

Lánchíd 19
MAP J4 ▪ I, Lánchíd utca 19 ▪ 06 1 457 12 00 ▪ www.lanchid19hotel. com ▪ FF
Situated on the Buda embankment, this modern "design hotel" features a unique glass façade, which changes colour during the evening. There are many stylish design touches inside, too. Rooms are large, equipped with lots of high-tech gizmos, and most have city views. The penthouse suites are simply dazzling.

art'otel
MAP H1 ▪ I, Bem rakpart 16–19 ▪ 06 1 487 94 87 ▪ www.artotels.com ▪ FFF
Situated in a sublime Neo-Baroque building on the banks of the Danube, this is a truly contem-porary hotel, inspired by modern art and design. Works by American artist Donald Sultan are on display, and the art concept covers everything from the carpets to the cutlery.

Budapest Marriott
MAP K4 ▪ V, Apáczai Csere János utca 4 ▪ 06 1 486 50 00 ▪ www.marriott. com/budhu ▪ FFF
The first of the five-star hotels in Budapest, the Marriott dates from 1969, and its architecture still stands out on the banks of the river Danube. All the rooms have stunning views.

Clark Hotel
MAP J3 ▪ I, Clark Ádám tér 1 ▪ 06 1 610 48 90 ▪ www.hotelclark budapest.hu ▪ FFF
Only adults are allowed admission at this luxu-rious hotel with fabulous views of Chain Bridge. The hotel is named after the Scottish engineer Adam Clark, who designed the bridge and the Buda Castle tunnel.

Four Seasons Hotel Gresham Palace
MAP K3 ▪ V, Széchenyi István tér 5–6 ▪ 06 1 268 60 00 ▪ www.four seasons.com ▪ FFF
The cost of staying at the city's most expen-sive hotel becomes insignificant as soon as you step into the foyer – it's a wonder of modern design in a classic setting. A Secession landmark, the Gresham Palace offers splendid service and views of the Chain Bridge, Danube and the Buda Hills (see p83).

InterContinental Budapest
MAP K3 ▪ V, Apáczai Csere János utca 12–14 ▪ 06 1 327 63 33 ▪ www. ihg.com ▪ FFF
Spacious rooms with windows overlooking the Danube are the main draw of this perennially popular hotel. The public reception areas are wel-coming, and the hotel's Corso restaurant gets excellent reviews, especially for the lavish Sunday brunch buffet.

Mid-Range and Apart-Hotels

Dominika Apartman Hotel
MAP N2 ▪ XII, Lidérc utca 13 ▪ 06 1 246 00 62 ▪ www.dominikahotel.hu ▪ F
At the cheap end of the apartment sector, these superb apartments are housed inside a guest-house in a leafy Budapest suburb. There's a terrace and a swimming pool at the back of the building.

Carlton Hotel
MAP H3 ▪ I, Apor Péter utca 3 ▪ 06 1 224 09 99 ▪ www.carltonhotel.hu ▪ FF
The austere-looking Carlton is a good mid-range hotel. Decor is rather basic, but all 95 rooms are comfortable and have air conditioning. An excellent buffet break-fast is included in the price of your room.

Corvin Hotel Sissi Wings
MAP P2 ▪ IX, Angyal utca 33 ▪ 06 1 218 65 66 ▪ www.corvinhotel budapest.hu ▪ FF
Named after Elizabeth (Erzsébet) – the wife of Emperor Franz József II – who was known to her friends as Sissi, this hotel is worthy of her name. It is a charming place with smart interiors and 44 large rooms, some of which have balconies. Several rooms are set aside as non-smoking.

Ibis Centrum
MAP M5 ▪ IX, Ráday utca 6 ▪ 06 1 456 41 00 ▪ www.ibis.com ▪ FF
Part of the Ibis chain, which offers a decent

level of accommodation at low prices. It's located on one of the busiest streets in town, but rooms are soundproofed from the noise below. There's a lovely garden patio.

Locust Tree Apartments
MAP D4 ■ VII, Akacfa utca 12 ■ 0670 394 26 51 ■ locusttree apartments.com ■ FF
Just a few minutes away from most of the popular attractions, this relaxed apartment hotel, on a busy street full of clubs, bars and cafés, offers cable TV, tea, coffee and a laundry service – all at a fair price.

Manzárd Panzió
MAP F6 ■ Bláthy Ottó utca 21 ■ 06 1 210 41 41 ■ www.manzardpanzio. com ■ FF
Located in a quiet residential area of downtown Budapest, the Manzárd Panzió is a charming and simple hotel. It has a large garden, provides free Wi-Fi access and arranges barbecue and goulash parties quite often.

City Gardens Apartment Hotel
MAP M1 ■ VI, Ó utca 43–49 ■ 0620 285 08 07 ■ www.citygardens budapest.com ■ FFF
All the mod cons you need – including a DVD library, tea- and coffee-making facilities and free Wi-Fi – make these apartments a viable alternative to traditional hotels. The building also has a gym and sauna for guests to use. Airport transfers can also be arranged when booking.

Budget Hotels

Adagio Hostel 2.0 Basilica
MAP C4 ■ VII, Andrássy út 2 ■ 06 1 950 96 74 ■ www. adagiohostel.com ■ F
This modern hostel has an enviable location on the city's most exclusive street. Reasonably priced private rooms and dorms, plus a host of facilities are offered, such as a laundry service.

Avenue Hostel
MAP D3 ■ VI, Oktogon 4 ■ 0670 410 61 35 ■ www. avenuehostel.hu ■ F
Within walking distance of sights like City Park and the Hungarian Parliament, this hostel offers great location on a budget. In addition to a mix of dorms and private rooms, it has a lively bar and café, which becomes a hub for travellers in the evenings.

Boat Hostel Fortuna
MAP C1 ■ XIII, Szent István Park, Alsó rakpart ■ 06 70 770 04 03 ■ www. fortunaboat.com ■ F
Most of this boat is part of a rather fine hotel, but there are also dorm rooms in the hull, which market themselves as a hostel. These are cheaper, though more crowded, than the hotel rooms.

Flow Spaces
MAP D5 ■ V, Gönczy Pál utca 2 ■ 0620 491 00 03 ■ www.flowhostel.hu ■ F
Set in an old, red-brick warehouse, the interiors at this hostel are wonderfully light and modern. There is a good range of private and shared rooms, all decorated in bright colours, and a handy work space.

Full Moon Hostel
MAP C2 ■ V, Szent István körút 11 ■ 06 1 792 90 45 ■ www.fullmoonhostel. com ■ F
Bright and colourful, with huge portraits of 1960s rock stars at every turn, this is a vibrant, late-night hostel. It offers decent accommodation in an assortment of options, including private rooms.

The Loft Hostel
MAP C5 ■ Veres Pálné utca 19 ■ 0630 957 89 57 ■ F
Quirky art adorns the walls of this simple but great value hostel. It is ideally located in an old Budapest courtyard block in the heart of the city's party district around Váci Street.

Maverick Urban Lodge
MAP D5 ■ V, Lónyay utca 31 ■ 06 1 472 52 32 ■ www.mavericklodges ■ F
A boutique spot that takes the hostel concept up a notch. Expect elegant common areas – including a workspace, modern kitchen, a rooftop bar and a street terrace – plus a range of comfortable private rooms and shared dorms.

Shantee House
MAP N2 ■ XI,Takács Menyhért utca 33 ■ 06 1 385 89 46 ■ www.back packbudapest.hu ■ F
Popular with young backpackers, this guesthouse is always buzzing. There's a courtyard, and while the rooms are basic, they are impeccably clean and have fresh linen daily. Air conditioning is not offered in the rooms.

For a key to hotel price categories see p114

General Index

Page numbers in **bold** refer to main entries

Acknowledgments

Author

A linguist by training, Craig Turp has authored many travel guides over the course of a career spanning more than two decades. He is currently the editor of Emerging Europe, a think tank and news website focused on social, economic, political and cultural issues in Central and Eastern Europe. He lives in Bucharest, Romania.

Publishing Director Georgina Dee

Publisher Vivien Antwi

Design Director Phil Ormerod

Editorial Michelle Crane, Rachel Fox, Fay Franklin, Priyanka Kumar, Sally Schafer, Hollie Teague, Sophie Wright

Cover Design Bess Daly, Maxine Pedliham

Design Hansa Babra, Tessa Bindloss, Rahul Kumar, Bhavika Mathur, Marisa Renzullo, Stuti Tiwari

Picture Research Ellen Root, Lucy Sienkowska, Rituraj Singh

Cartography Subhashree Bharti, Uma Bhattacharya, James Macdonald, Casper Morris

DTP Jason Little, Azeem Siddiqui

Production Che Creasey

Factchecker Krisztián R. Hildebrand

Proofreader Susanne Hillen

Indexer Helen Peters

Revisions Parnika Bagla, Subhashree Bharati, Mohammad Hassan, Krisztián R. Hildebrand, Sumita Khatwani, Shikha Kulkarni, Rachel Laidler, Halima Mohammed, Anjasi Nongkynrih Nyshadham, Rohit Rojal, Beverly Smart, Mark Silas, Manjari Thakur, Stuti Tiwari, Vaishali Vashisht, Vinita Venugopal

Commissioned Photography Demetrio Carrasco, Rough Guides/Eddie Gerald

Picture Credits

Hungarian Arts & Crafts Festival: 62br.

Hungarian National Assembly: 15bl; Mark Mervai 12bl.

Hungarian National Museum: 34tr, 34cla,34br, 35tll, 35crb.

Hungarian State Opera: Attila Juha 32cla; Attila Juhasz 32-3, 33tl; Attila Nagy 32br; 82br.

iStockphoto.com: ZoltanGabor 1.

Kassák Museum: 104cla.

Magnolia Day Spa: 48tr.

Mary Evans Picture Library: 40bl.

Memories of Hungary: 59cr.

Museum of Fine Arts Budapest: Gyula Benczúr *The Recapture of Buda Castle* 1896 26cl; Károly Ferenczy *Birdsong* 1667 27tc; Lajos Gulácsy *The Garden of the Magician* 1906-1907/Fehér Katalin 29c; Master MS *The Visitation* 1500-1510 26tr; Mihály Munkácsy *The Yawning Apprentice* 1869/Mester Tibor 26crb; József Rippl-Rónai *Woman in a White-Spotted Dress* 1898 28tc; József Rippl-Rónai *The Manor House at Körtyvelyes* 1907/Berényi Zsuzsa 28bl; János Vaszary *Fancy Dress Ball* 1907 28crb.

Oscar American Cocktail Bar: 72cla.

Ötkert: Soós Bertalan 84cl.

Palack Borbar: 79cra.

Rex by Shutterstock: Colorsport 102br; N 51cr.

Robert Harding Picture Library: Stuart Black 70tl; Peter Erik Forsberg 71cla; Eduardo Grund 97cl; Carlo Morucchio 43cr; Ingolf Pompe 90bl.

SuperStock: age fotostock/Domingo Leiva Nicolas 10crb; imageBROKER 22cla, / Matthias Hauser 23br.

Sziget: Sa ándoľ Csuuui ÓÌ́ì.

Szimpla Kert: 56cl.

Törley Museum: 101cla.

WAMP - Design in the City: 59br.

Wekerle Community Association: Miklós; dr.Toldy 104br.

Cover:

Front and spine: **iStockphoto.com:** ZoltanGabor.

Back: **Alamy Stock Photo:** Yury Kirillov cla; **Dreamstime.com:** Olga Lupol tl; William Perry crb; Rudi1976 tr, **iStockphoto.com:** ZoltanGabor b.

Pull Out Map Cover:

iStockphoto.com: ZoltanGabor.

All other images © Dorling Kindersley

For further information see:
www.dkimages.com

DK | Penguin Random House

First Edition 2006

First published in Great Britain
by Dorling Kindersley Limited
DK, One Embassy Gardens, 8 Viaduct
Gardens, London SW11 7BW, UK

The authorised representative in the EEA is
Dorling Kindersley Verlag GmbH. Arnulfstr.
124, 80636 Munich, Germany

Published in the United States by
DK Publishing, 1745 Broadway, 20th Floor,
New York, NY 10019, USA

Copyright © 2006, 2022 Dorling
Kindersley Limited
A Penguin Random House Company

23 24 25 10 9 8 7 6 5 4 3

**Reprinted with revisions 2008, 2010,
2012, 2014, 2017, 2019, 2022**

All rights reserved.

A CIP catalogue record is available
from the British Library.

A catalogue record for this book is
available from the Library of Congress.

ISSN 1479-344X

ISBN 978-0-24146-286-7

Printed and bound in Malaysia

www.dk.com

*As a guide to abbreviations in visitor information
blocks:* **Adm** = admission charge; **D** = dinner.

MIX
Paper | Supporting
responsible forestry
FSC
www.fsc.org   FSC™ C018179

This book was made with Forest
Stewardship Council™ certified
paper – one small step in DK's
commitment to a sustainable future.
**For more information go to
www.dk.com/our-green-pledge**

Phrase Book

In an Emergency

Help!	Segítség!	shegeetshayg!
Stop!	Stop!	shtop!
Call a doctor	Hívjon orvost!	heevyon orvosht!
Call an ambulance	Hívjon mentőt!	heevyon menturt
Call the police	Hívja a rendőrséget	heevya a rendur shayget
Call the fire department	Hívja a tűzoltókat!	heevya a tewzoltowkot!
Where is the nearest telephone?	Hol van a legközelebbi telefon?	hol von uh legkurze-lebbi telefon?
Where is the nearest hospital?	Hol van a legközelebbi kórház?	hol von a leg-kurze-lebbi koorhahz?

Communications Essentials

Yes/No	Igen/Nem	igen/nem
Please (offering)	Tessék	teshayk
Please (asking)	Kérem	kayrem
Thank you	Köszönöm	kurss urnurm
No, thank you	Köszönöm nem	kurss urnurm nem
Excuse me, please	Bocsánatot kérek	bochanutot kayrek
Hello	Jó napot	yow nopot
Goodbye	Viszontlátásra	vissont-latashruh
What?	Mi?	mi?
When?	Mikor?	mikor?
Why?	Miért?	miayrt?
Where?	Hol?	hol?

Useful Phrases

How are you?	Hogy van?	hod-yuh vun?
Very well, thank you	köszönöm nagyon jól	kurss urnurm nojjon yowl
Pleased to meet you	Örülök hogy megismerhettem	ur-rewlurk hod-yuh megish-merhettem
Where can I get…?	Hol kaphatok …-t?	hol kuphutok …-t?
How do you get to?	Hogy lehet …-ba eljutni?	hod-yuh lehet …-buh el-yootni?
Do you speak English?	Beszél angolul?	bessayl ungolool?
I can't speak Hungarian	Nem beszélek magyarul	nem bessaylek mud-yarool
I don't understand	Nem értem	nem ayrtem
Can you help me?	Kérhetem a segítségét?	kayrhetem uh sheg-eechaygayt
Please speak slowly	Tessék lassabban beszélni	teshayk lushubbun bessaylni
Sorry!	Elnézést!	elnayzaysht!

Useful Words

big	nagy	noj
small	kicsi	kichi
hot	forró	forow
cold	hideg	hideg
good	jó	yow
bad	rossz	ross
open	nyitva	nyitva
closed	zárva	zarva
left	bal	bol
right	jobb	yob
entrance	bejárat	beh-yarut
exit	kijárat	ki-yarut

toilet	WC	vaytsay
free/unoccupied	szabad	sobbod
free/no charge	ingyen	injen

Making a Telephone Call

Can I call abroad from here?	Telefonálhatok innen külföldre?	telefonalhutok inen kewlfurldreh?
Could I leave a message?	Hagyhatnék egy üzenetet?	hud-yuhutnayk ed-yuh ewzenetet?
Hold on	Várjon!	vahr-yon!

Shopping

How much is this?	Ez mennyibe kerül?	ez menn-yibeh kerewl?
Do you have…?	Kapható önöknél…?	kuphutaw urnurknayl…?
Do you take credit cards?	Elfogadják a hitelkártyákat?	elfogud-yak uh hitelkart-yakut?
What time do you open/close?	Hánykor nyitnak/zárnak?	Hahn kor nyitnak/zárnak?
this one	ez	ez
expensive	drága	drahga
cheap	olcsó	olchow
size	méret	mayret
white	fehér	feheer
black	fekete	feketeh
red	piros	pirosh
yellow	sárga	sharga
green	zöld	zurld
blue	kék	cake
brown	barna	borna

Types of Shop

antiques dealer	régiségkeres-kedő	ray-gee-shayg-kereshk-kedur
bank	bank	bonk
bookshop	könyvesbolt	kurn-yuveshbolt
cake shop	cukrászda	tsookrassduh
chemist	patika	putikuh
department store	áruház	aroo-haz
florist	virágüzlet	virag-ewzlet
food store	élelmiszerbolt	ail-ell-miss-er
market	piac	pi-uts
newsagent	újságos	oo-yushagosh
post office	postahivatal	poshta-hivatal
shoe shop	cipőbolt	tsipurbolt
souvenir shop	ajándékbolt	uy-yandaykbolt
tobacconist	trafik	trafik
travel agent	utazási iroda	ootuzashi iroduh

Sightseeing

bus	autóbusz	owtawbooss
tram	villamos	villumosh
train	vonat	vonut
underground	metró	metraw
bus stop	buszmegálló	booss megallaw
art gallery	képcsarnok	kayp-chornok
palace	palota	polola
church	templom	templom
garden	kert	kert
library	könyvtár	kurnvtar
museum	múzeum	moozayoom
tourist information	túristahivatal	toorishta-hivotol
closed for public holiday	ünnepnap zárva	ewn-nepnap zarva

Staying in a Hotel

Have you any vacancies?	Van kiadó szobájuk?	vun ki-udaw soba-yook?
double room with double bed	francia-ágyas szoba	frontsia-ahjosh sobuh
twin room	kétágyas szoba	kaytad-yush sobuh
single room	egyágyas szoba	ed-yad-yush sobuh
room with a bath/shower	fürdőszobás/zuhanyzós szoba	fewrdur-sobahsh/zoo-honzahsh soba
porter	portás	portahsh
key	kulcs	koolch
I have a reservation	Foglaltam egy szobát	foglultum ed-yuh sobat

Eating Out

A table for… please	Egy asztalt szeretnék… személyre	ed-yuh usstult seretnayk… semayreh
I want to reserve a table	Szeretnék egy asztalt foglalni	seretnayk ed-yuh usstult foglolni
The bill please	Kérem a számlát	kayrem uh samlat
I am a vegetarian	Vegetáriánus vagyok	vegetariahnoosh vojok
I'd like…	Szeretnék-egy…-t	seret nayk ed-yuh…-t
waiter/ waitress	pincér/ pincérnő	pintsayr/ pintsayrnur
menu	étlap	aytlup
wine list	borlap	bohrlup
drinks menu	itallap	itallup
glass	pohár	pohar
bottle	üveg	ewveg
knife	kés	kaysh
fork	villa	villuh
spoon	kanál	kunal
breakfast	reggeli	reg-geli
lunch	ebéd	ebayd
dinner	vacsora	vochora
main courses	főételek	fur-aytelek
starters	előételek	elur-aytelek
desserts	desszertek	dess-air-tekh
rare	angolosan	ongoloshan
well done	átsütve	ahtshewtveh

Menu Decoder

ásványvíz	ahshvahnveez	mineral water
bárány	bahrahn	lamb
bors	borsh	pepper
csirke	cheerkeh	chicken
csokoládé	chokolahday	chocolate
cukor	tsookor	sugar
ecet	etset	vinegar
fagylalt	fodyuhloot	ice cream
fehérbor	feheerbor	white wine
fokhagyma	fokhodyuhma	garlic
főtt	furt	boiled
gomba	gomba	mushrooms
gyümölcs	dyewmurlch	fruit
gyümölcslé	dyewmurlch-lay	fruit juice
hagyma	hojma	onions
hal	hol	fish
hús	hoosh	meat
kávé	kavay	coffee
kenyér	ken-yeer	bread
krumpli	kroompli	potatoes
kolbász	kolbahss	sausage
leves	levesh	soup
marha	marha	beef
mustár	mooshtahr	mustard
paradicsom	porodichom	tomatoes
párolt	pahrolt	steamed
rizs	rizh	rice
bifsztek	bifstek	steak
roston	roshton	grilled
sajt	shoyt	cheese
saláta	sholahta	salad
sertéshús	shertaysh-hoosh	pork
só	shaw	salt
sonka	shonka	ham
sör	shur	beer
sült	shewlt	fried/roasted
sült burgonya	shewlt boorgonya	chips
sütemény	shewtemayn-yuh	cake, pastry
tea	tay-uh	tea
tej	tay	milk
tejszín	taysseen	cream
tengeri hal	tengeri hol	sea fish
tojás	toyahsh	egg
vörösbor	vur-rurshbor	red wine
zsemle	zhemleh	roll
zsemlegom-bóc	zhemlehgom-bowts	dumplings

Numbers

0	nulla	noolluh
1	egy	ed-yuh
2	kettő, két	kettur, kayt
3	három	harom
4	négy	nayd-yuh
5	öt	urt
6	hat	hut
7	hét	hayt
8	nyolc	n-yolts
9	kilenc	kilents
10	tíz	teez
11	tizenegy	tizened-yuh
12	tizenkettő	tizenkettur
13	tizenhárom	tizenharom
14	tizennégy	tizen-nayd-yuh
15	tizenöt	tizenurt
16	tizenhat	tizenhut
17	tizenhét	tizenhayt
18	tizennyolc	tizenn-yolts
19	tizenkilenc	tizenkilents
20	húsz	hooss
30	harminc	hurmints
40	negyven	ned-yuven
50	ötven	urtven
60	hatvan	hutvun
70	hetven	hetven
80	nyolcvan	n-yoltsvun
90	kilencven	kilentsven
100	száz	saz
1,000	ezer	ezer
10,000	tízezer	teezezer
1,000,000	millió	milliaw

Time

one minute	egy perc	ed-yuh perts
hour	óra	awruh
half an hour	félóra	faylawruh
Sunday	vasárnap	vusharnup
Monday	hétfő	haytfur
Tuesday	kedd	kedd
Wednesday	szerda	serduh
Thursday	csütörtök	chewturturk
Friday	péntek	payntek
Saturday	szombat	sombut

Selected Budapest Street Index